THE JOHN DEWEY LECTURE

The John Dewey Lecture is delivered annually under the sponsorship of the John Dewey Society. The intention of the series is to provide a setting where able thinkers from various sectors of our intellectual life can direct their most searching thought to problems that involve the relation of education to culture. Arrangements for the presentation of the Lecture and its publication by Teachers College Press are under the direction of James M. Giarelli, Chairperson.

# Cultural Politics and Education

MICHAEL W. APPLE

Teachers College, Columbia University
New York and London

Published by Teachers College Press, 1234 Amsterdam Avenue, New York, NY 10027

*Library of Congress Cataloging-in-Publication Data*

Apple, Michael W.
    Cultural politics and education / by Michael W. Apple.
      p.    cm. — (The John Dewey lecture)
    Includes bibliographical references and index.
    ISBN 0-8077-3504-3 (cloth). — ISBN 0-8077-3503-5 (pbk.)
    1. Education—Political aspects—United States.  2. Critical
pedagogy—United States.  3. Education—Social aspects—United
States.  I. Title.  II. Series: John Dewey lecture (Columbia
University. Teachers College. Press)
LC89.A14  1996
370.19′2′0973—dc20                      95-36212

ISBN 0-8077-3503-5 (paper)
ISBN 0-8077-3504-3 (cloth)
Printed on acid-free paper
Manufactured in the United States of America
03  02  01  00  99  98  97  96     8  7  6  5  4  3  2

# Contents

# *Foreword*

John Dewey once wrote that "the objective precondition of the complete and free use of the method of intelligence is a society in which class interests that recoil from social experimentation are abolished. It is incompatible with every social and political philosophy and activity and with every economic system which accepts the class organization and vested class interest of society."[1]

Both the form and substance of Dewey's analysis display the classic characteristics of what is appropriately called a public philosophy of education. Over a lifetime of work Dewey continuously urged a form of educational inquiry in which the problems of the formation and re-formation of public life were understood by thinking *relationally* about the linkages between the economy, politics, culture, and schooling, whereas professional models of educational inquiry begin, and usually end, in distinctions.

In *Cultural Politics and Education*, Michael W. Apple once again demonstrates his preeminence as a practitioner of this critical tradition of progressive and public educational scholarship. Begun as the John Dewey Lecture of 1992, *Cultural Politics and Education* focuses on understanding the historically situated continuities and mediated tensions between the global and local consequences of international corporate capitalism, the growth and formation of conservative state and social movements, and the rhetoric and reality of specific curricular and school "reform" policies. Apple's analysis itself, which draws with sympathetic discrimination from both structuralist and various postmodern approaches, models a form of educational inquiry grounded in the creative relation of theoretical traditions. At its center, *Cultural Politics and Education* keeps a steady gaze on the problems of theorizing and practicing enabling forms of public education in a world of both celebrated and perniciously enforced differences.

Perhaps the central claim of all critical educational studies is that all true educational theories are theories of democracy and all true democratic theories are theories of education. Michael Apple restates this claim with an original voice; a voice of rigorous analysis and compassionate concern. *Cultural Politics and Education* is an invaluable book for all of us who consider ourselves public educators.

*James M. Giarelli*
Co-Chair, John Dewey Lecture Commission


NOTE

1. John Dewey, ''The Underlying Philosophy of Education,'' in William H. Kilpatrick, Ed., *The Educational Frontier* (pp. 316–317). The Century Co., 1933, New York and London.

# *Preface*

Authors are not mechanically determined by ideology, or class, or history. However, authors are very much *in* the history of their societies, "shaping and shaped by that history and their social experience."[1] This is certainly true of this author and this book.

I write this in the midst of many tensions and tendencies swirling around me. Books sometimes write authors as much as authors write books. This one is a bit of both. The book started out as an outline for the John Dewey Lecture that I was invited to give by the John Dewey Society and subsequently was presented as an address at AERA and Teachers College, Columbia University. I first saw my task as twofold: solidifying the arguments I had made about conservative tendencies in education and the larger society in *Official Knowledge*[2] and extending them to deal more specifically with the proposals for national curricula, national testing, and marketized "choice" plans in the United States. I am deeply troubled by these supposed reforms. While *Cultural Politics and Education* does accomplish these two tasks, as is often the case what I had to do soon became more complicated.

No one individual, and certainly not I, can fully grasp all of the complexity of education. While this book stands by itself as a statement of my understanding today, it also represents "simply" a continuation of my struggle—aided by and in concert with many others—to comprehend and challenge the prevailing ways education is carried on in this society. In this regard, its immediate parent is *Official Knowledge*, but the lineage of the questions it asks is easily found in *Ideology and Curriculum*, *Education and Power*, and *Teachers and Texts*.[3]

I began this book at a time when I had just returned from spending time in a Bosnian refugee camp populated by people (mostly women and children) who had somehow managed to flee the murderous situation there. What I saw in the camp and the stories the mostly Moslem Bosnian teachers told me, left me with a residue of anger that will never be erased. I also was left with a feeling of gratitude and awe as an educator. For in the midst of privations, fear, despair, and uncommon courage, one of the first acts of the people in that camp was to create a school for their children. It was a powerful reminder of how important education is to the maintenance of self and community and to what Raymond Williams so brilliantly called our journey of hope.[4]

Most important for the arguments in this volume, that journey of hope is not made any easier by the fact that this book is written at a time when the Right is resurgent, when it seems as if we basically have two right-wing parties in the United States, and when education and so much else is talked about as if all that counted was either competition and profit or a thoroughly romanticized return to the "Western tradition." As I write these words, rightist religious fundamentalism continues to grow and to have a greater influence on electoral politics, on social policy, and on what teachers will and will not teach in schools. The same is true about the growth of racist nativism. Such racist discourse is not limited to public debates about, say, immigration. The fact that the pseudo-science of Richard Herrnstein and Charles Murray in *The Bell Curve*[5] is currently being treated to such sponsored mobility—even though it is utterly naive in its understanding of genetics and both overtly and covertly racist in its arguments—creates a horizon against which my own writing here is constructed. All too many of us seem to have become inured to human suffering nationally and internationally. This is a difficult period for anyone who is committed to progressive social and educational transformation.

It is a complicated and tense period intellectually as well. From the Right, the culture wars rage. Yet, equally important, this book is written when postmodern and poststructural theories are becoming more influential in cultural studies and in critical educational studies (a label I would prefer to use rather than the more limited one of critical theory or critical pedagogy). There are significant parts of what my friends call "postie" approaches that are very insightful and need very close attention—especially their focus on identity politics, on multiple and contradictory relations of power, on nonreductive analysis, and on the local as an important site of struggle. The influence of some of this will be readily visible in this book. I have no wish at all to widen a divide when alliances are crucial now. However, there are also significant parts of these approaches as they have been introduced into education that make me blanch because of their stylistic arrogance, their stereotyping of other approaches and their concomitant certainty that they've got "the" answer, their cynical lack of attachment to any action in real schools, their seeming equation of any serious focus on the economy as being somehow reductive, their conceptual confusions, and, finally, their trendy rhetoric that when unpacked often says some pretty commonsensical things that reflexive educators have known and done for years. Let me hasten to add that this is true for only a portion of these approaches, but all of this gives me cause for concern. [6]

Thus, there is a fine line between necessary conceptual and political transformations and trendiness. Unfortunately, the latter sometimes appears in the relatively uncritical appropriation of postmodernism by some educational theorists. For example, there certainly are (too many) plans to turn schools over to market forces, to diversify types of schools and give "consumers" more choice. Some may argue that this is "the educational equivalent of . . . the rise of 'flexible specialization in place of the old assembly-line world of mass production,' driven by the imperatives of differentiated consumption rather than mass production." [7] This certainly has a postmodern ring to it.

Yet, like many of the new reforms being proposed, there is less that is "postmodern" about them than meets the eye. Many have a "high-tech" image. They usually are guided by "an underlying faith in technical rationality as the basis for solving social, economic, and educational problems." Specialization is just as powerful as, perhaps even more powerful than, any concern for diversity. [8] Rather than an espousal of "heterogeneity, pluralism, and the local"—although these may be the rhetorical forms in which some of these reforms are couched—what we may actually be witnessing is the revivification of more traditional class, gender, and especially race hierarchies. An unquestioning commitment to the notion that "we" are now fully involved in a postmodern world may make it easier to see surface transformations (some of which are undoubtedly occurring) and yet at the same time may make it that much more difficult to recognize that these may be new ways of reorganizing and reproducing older hierarchies. [9] The fact that parts of postmodernism as a theory and as a set of experiences may not be applicable to an extremely large portion of the world's population should make us a bit more cautious as well.

As you read this book, it will become clear that part, though certainly not all, of what I say here is based on a critical (and self-critical) structural understanding of education. While not economically reductive, it does require that we recognize that we live under capitalist relations. Milton Friedman and the entire gamut of privatizers and marketizers who have so much influence in the media and the corridors of power in corporate board rooms, foundations, and our government at nearly all levels spend considerable amounts of time praising these relations. If they can talk about them, why can't we? These relations *don't* determine everything. They are constituted out of and reconstituted by race, class, and gender relations, but it seems a bit naive to ignore them. There is a world of difference between taking economic power and structures seriously and reducing everything down to a pale reflection of them.

I am fully cognizant that there are many dangers in such an approach. It has as part of its history attempts to create a "grand narrative," a theory that explains everything based on a unitary cause. It also tends to make us forget that not only are there multiple and contradictory relations of power in nearly every situation, but the researcher herself or himself is a participant in such relations. [10] Finally, structural approaches at times can neglect the ways our discourses are constructed out of, and themselves help construct, what we do. These indeed are issues that need to be taken seriously. Poststructural and postmodern criticisms of structural analyses in education have been fruitful in this regard, especially when they have arisen from within the various feminist and postcolonial communities, [11] although it must be said that some of these criticisms have created wildly inaccurate caricatures of the neo-Marxist traditions.

Yet, even though the "linguistic turn," as it has been called in sociology and cultural studies, has been immensely productive, it is important to remember that the world of education and elsewhere is not only a text. There are gritty realities out there, realities whose power often is grounded in structural relations that are not simply social constructions created by the meanings given by an observer. Part of our task, it seems to me, is to not lose sight of these gritty realities in the economy and the state, while at the same time recognizing the dangers of essentializing and reductive analyses.

My point is not to deny that many elements of "postmodernity" exist, nor is it to deny the power of certain aspects of postmodern theory. Rather, it is to avoid overstatement, to avoid substituting one grand narrative for another—a grand narrative that actually never existed in the United States, since class and economy only recently surfaced in critical educational scholarship and only rarely were seen here in the form found in Europe, where most postmodern and poststructural criticisms of these explanatory tools were developed. It would help if we remembered that the intellectual and political histories of the United States were very different from those castigated by some postmodern critics. Reductive analysis comes cheap, and there is no guarantee that postmodern positions, as currently employed by some in education, are any more immune to this danger than is any other position.

Thus, in this book it will not be a surprise that side by side with poststructural and postmodern understandings are those based on structural theories. While they are not totally merged, each one serves as a corrective and complement to the other. This is a point I wish to emphasize. Rather than spending so much time treating each other so warily—sometimes as enemies—we should view the creative tension that exists as a good thing. We have a good deal to learn from each other in terms of a politics in and around education that makes a difference (no pun is intended here).

There are a number of other intellectual tensions that swirl around this book. As I reflect on the growth of certain styles of doing critical analysis in education, it is clear that there has been a rapid growth of two other kinds of work: personal/literary/autobiographical analyses and studies of popular culture. The former often have been stimulated by phenomenological, psychoanalytic, and feminist approaches. The latter have arisen from cultural studies. Let me say something about each of these.

Much of the impetus behind personal stories is moral. Education is seen correctly as an ethical enterprise. The personal is seen as a way to reawaken ethical and aesthetic sensitivities that, increasingly, have been purged from the scientistic discourse of too many educators. Or it is seen as a way of giving a voice to the subjectivities of people who have been silenced. There is much to commend in this position. Indeed, any approach that evacuates the aesthetic, the personal, and the ethical from our activities as educators is not about education at all. It is about training. Yet something remains a little too much in the background in many variants of such stories—a biting sense of the political, of the social structures that condemn so many identifiable people to lives of economic and cultural (and bodily) struggle and, at times, despair. Making connections between what might be called the literary imagination and the concrete movements—in both education *and* the larger society—that seek to transform our institutions so that caring and social justice are not just slogans but realities, is essential here. Political arguments are not alternatives to moral and aesthetic concerns. Rather, they are these concerns taken seriously, with an appreciation of their full implications.[12] And this leads me to raise a caution about some of the hidden effects of our (generally commendable) urge to employ the personal and the autobiographical to illuminate our (admittedly differential) educational experiences.

For nearly 20 years, until the publication of *Official Knowledge*, I did not write about my experiences as a film maker with teachers and students, in part because I could not find an appropriate "voice." It would have required a fair dose of autobiography. I often find autobiographical accounts and narrative renderings compelling and insightful, and do not want in any way to dismiss their power in educational theory and practice. Yet—and let me be blunt here—just as often such writing runs the risk of lapsing into what has been called possessive individualism.[13] Even when an author does the "correct thing" and discusses her or his social location in a world dominated by oppressive conditions, such writing can serve the chilling function of simply saying, "But enough about you, let me tell you about me," unless we are much more reflexive about this than often has been the case. I am still committed enough to raising questions about class dynamics to worry about perspectives that supposedly acknowledge the missing voices of many people in our thinking about education, but still wind up privileging the white, middle class woman's or man's need for *self-display*.

Do not misconstrue what I am saying here. As so much feminist and postcolonial work has documented, the personal often is the absent presence behind even the most eviscerated writing, and we do need to continue to explore ways of heightening the sense of the personal in our "stories" about education. But, at the same time, it is equally crucial that we interrogate our own "hidden" motives here. Is the insistence on the personal, an insistence that underpins much of our turn to literary and autobiographical forms, partly a class discourse as well? The "personal may be the political," but does the political end at the personal? Furthermore, why should we assume that the personal is any less difficult to understand than the "external" world? I cannot answer these questions for all situations, but I think that these questions must be asked by all of us who are committed to the multiple projects involved in struggling for a more emancipatory education. For this very reason, I open the first chapter in this book with a personal story that is *consciously* connected to a clear sense of the realities of structurally generated inequalities that play such a large role in education.

My intellectual/political tensions do not end here, however. "Boom times" in academic stocks and bonds come and go.[14] In some parts of the critical educational community, the study of popular culture—music, dance, films, language, dress, bodily transformations, the politics of consumption, and so on—is also big business. And in many ways it should be. After all, we should know by now that popular culture is *partly* a site of resistance and struggle,[15] but also that for schooling to make a difference it must connect to popular understandings and cultural forms. Yet, our fascination with "the popular," our intoxication with all of these things, has sometimes had a paradoxical and unfortunate effect. It often has led us to ignore the actual knowledge that *is* taught in schools, the entire corpus and structure of the formal processes of curriculum, teaching, and evaluation that remain so powerful. In many ways, it constitutes a flight from education as a field. In my more cynical moments, I take this as a class discourse in which new elements within the academy in education fight for power not only over school folks but over positions within the academy itself.

Later on in this book, I shall talk about the importance of popular culture and shall make a plea for its centrality both in understanding cultural politics and in struggling to institute more socially just models of curriculum and teaching. Yet, many members of the critical educational community have been a bit too trendy about this topic as well. They seem to have forgotten about schools, curricula, teachers, students, community activists, and so on. It's as if dealing with these issues is "polluting," as if they are afraid of getting their hands dirty with the daily realities of education. Or perhaps they feel that it's not theoretically elegant enough to deal with such "mundane" realities. While I fully understand the utter necessity of focusing on the popular, as a critical *educator* I am even more committed to taking seriously the reality of school matters.[16] For this very reason, *Cultural Politics and Education* devotes much of its attention to matters specifically related to the politics of curriculum and teaching.

I do not want to be overly negative here. Many of us have quite ambivalent feelings about the place called school. All of us who care deeply about what is and is not taught, and about who is and is not empowered to deal with these issues, have a contradictory relationship to these institutions. We want to criticize them rigorously and yet in this very criticism lies a commitment, a hope, that they can be made more vital, more personally meaningful and socially critical. If ever there was a love/hate relationship, this is it.[17] This speaks directly to the situation many people in critical educational studies face today and underlies some of the emphases of this book.

The New Right is very powerful now. It has had the odd effect of simultaneously interrupting the progressive critique of schooling while leading many of us to defend an institution many of whose practices were and are open to severe criticism.[18] As someone who has devoted years to analyzing and acting on the social and cultural means and ends of our curricula, teaching, and evaluation in schools, I certainly do not want to act as an apologist for poor practices. Yet, during an era when—because of rightist attacks—we face the massive dismantling of the gains (limited as they are) that have been made in social welfare, in women's control of their bodies, in relations of race, gender, and sexuality, and in whose knowledge is taught in schools, it is equally important to make certain that these gains are defended.

Thus, there is another clear tension in this volume. I want to both defend the idea of a *public* education, and a number of the gains that do exist, and at the same time to criticize many of its attributes. This dual focus may seem a bit odd at first, but it speaks to a crucial point I want to make about how we should think about the institutions of formal education in most of our nations.

Here I want to say something that may make a number of educators who are justifiably critical of existing power relations in education a bit uncomfortable. The problem I shall point to may at first seem minor, but its conceptual, political, and practical implications are not. I am referring to the discourse of *change.* This discourse stands behind all of those claims about both the autobiographical and popular culture and behind the pressures to connect schools more closely to economic needs and goals. All too often we forget that in our attempts to alter and "reform" schooling there are elements that should not be changed but need to be kept and defended. Even with my criticisms of the unequal power relations surrounding education and the larger society, we need to remember that schooling never was simply an imposition on supposedly politically/culturally inept people. Rather, as I have demonstrated elsewhere, educational policies and practices were and are the result of struggles and compromises over what would count as legitimate knowledge, pedagogy, goals, and criteria for determining effectiveness. In a more abstract way, we can say that education has been one of the major arenas in which the conflict between property rights and person rights has been fought. [19]

The results of these conflicts have not always been settled on the terms of dominant groups. Often, democratic tendencies have emerged and have been cemented into the daily practices of the institution. As William Reese shows in his history of populist reform in schools, many things that we take for granted were the direct results of populist movements that forced powerful groups to compromise, and even to suffer outright losses. [20] Thus, before we give a blanket condemnation to what schools do and turn to what we suppose is the alternative (say, popular culture), we need a much clearer and more historically informed appraisal of what elements of the practices and policies of these institutions are already progressive and should be maintained. Not to do so would be to assume that, say, radical teachers, people of color, women, working class groups, and physically challenged groups (these categories obviously are not mutually exclusive) have been puppets whose strings are pulled by the most conservative forces in this society and have not won any lasting victories in education. This simply is not the case. Not to defend some of the ideas behind person rights that are currently embodied in schools is to add more power to conservative attacks.

I do not want to belabor this point, but it does make a major difference in how we approach education. At times, some critical educators have been so critical that we too often assume—consciously or unconsciously—that everything that exists within the educational system bears only the marks of domination. It's all capitalist; it's all racist; it's all patriarchal; it's all homophobic. As you would imagine given my own efforts over the past 3 decades, I do not want to dismiss the utter power of these and other forms of oppression in education or in anything else. Yet, in taking a stance that *assumes*—without detailed investigation—that all is somehow the result of relations of dominance, we also make it very difficult to make connections with progressive educators and community members who currently are struggling to build an education that is democratic in more than name only. (And there are many practicing educators who have been more than a little successful in such struggles.) It is all too easy for critical educators to fall into this position.

This assumption is problematic conceptually, historically, and politically. It rests on a theory of the role of state institutions that is too simplistic and on an ahistorical understanding of the power of democratically inclined groups.[21] It also bears the marks of what seems like a form of self-hatred, as if the more we distance ourselves from the history and discourse of education—and turn to other, "more academically respectable," fields for all of our perspectives—the more academically legitimate we become. The ultimate effects of this are disabling for any of us who wish to continue the long and essential struggle to have our educational institutions respond to the needs of not only the powerful.

This is a difficult tightrope to walk for those of us involved in education. In a time of right-wing resurgence, how do we create the educational conditions in which our students can see (and teach us about as well) the very real and massive relations of inequality and the role of schooling in partly reproducing and contesting them, and at the same time jointly create the conditions that assist all of us in empowering each other to act on these realities? Gramsci had a way of saying it: Pessimism of the intellect, optimism of the will. But my point goes well beyond this. Intellect, enlivened by passion and ethical/political sensitivities—and a fine sense of historical agency—will see victories as well as losses, hope as well as despair. That, it seems to me, is our task.

Finally, and this is directly related to what I have just said, there has been one other tension behind this book. When I began writing this volume, not only did I want to both criticize and defend much that is happening in education, I also wanted to illuminate what it actually *is* that needs to be defended. What policies and practices now exist in schools and classrooms that are socially and educationally critical? Are there what elsewhere I have called crucial "nonreformist reforms" that need to be continued?[22] This has caused me no end of headaches. While throughout this book I shall refer to such policies and practices, for political and ethical reasons (and perhaps for reasons of sanity) I decided that extensive descriptions of such critical practice clearly deserved an entire book of their own. Furthermore, they should be written by the educator-activists who actually engage in them, in their own words. Because of this, while it is not totally a companion volume, in the usual sense of that concept, to the one you are reading, at the same time that I was writing this book my colleague and friend Jim Beane and I produced such a book—*Democratic Schools*.[23] It details in much greater depth what is possible in public schools now.

This has been a slightly cranky Preface. But what follows is a "reading" of the current realities confronting educators. Thus, it is important that you know the multiple concerns that formed the lenses through which you will be asked to look at the politics surrounding the current world of education. The problems to which these concerns speak—some personal, some conceptual, and some political—will not be totally "solved" in this book. At times, I felt like a juggler trying to keep multiple balls in the air. If I drop one here and there—well, I'm certain that enough readers will let me know and, I hope, will assist me in picking them up.

## ACKNOWLEDGMENTS

Fortunately, I have already received a good deal of assistance from individuals in many countries. One of the things I ask of friends and colleagues is constructive criticism. The last thing any of us needs are acolytes who simply agree with everything we say. In fact, rather than seeing it as a treasonable act, constructive criticism should be viewed as the mark that your position has been taken seriously. There are a number of people who have helped me see things that I might not have and a number of institutions that have provided a formative context in which such conversations could go on.

For 25 years, I have taught at the University of Wisconsin, Madison. It continues to be a special place. Political differences, beliefs about what education now does, what it should do, and how it should be carried out, and about one's understandings of what research is for, are quite divergent here in Madison. Yet, these differences rarely surface in unhealthy ways. Critical work has never been marginalized and in many ways is the norm here. In this regard, I would like to acknowledge the financial assistance of the Graduate School Research Fund at the University of Wisconsin, Madison for its financial support for parts of this volume.

Outside of Wisconsin, the arguments in this book were first presented at various universities and academic and political forums throughout the world. Although these are too numerous to name, you know who you are and I want to thank you for your critical comments. There are four institutions that do need to be noted, however, since I have had repeated connections with faculty and students there. They too have been special places where I have worked through these arguments in public and private conversations. These are the University of Trondheim, the University of Auckland, the University of Ljubljana, and the Universidad Nacional Autonoma de Mexico.

Institutions are made up of people and I have benefited from the critical support of the following individuals: Petter Aasen, Alicia de Alba, Peter Apple, Eva Bahovec, Len Barton, Basil Bernstein, Thomas Carpenter, Kathleen Casey, Lourdes Chehaibar, Seehwa Cho, John Codd, Bob Connell, Roger Dale, Ann DeVaney, Mariano Fernandez Enguita, Walter Feinberg, Elizabeth Fenemma, James Giarelli, David Gillbourn, Edgar Gonzales, Liz Gordon, Jenny Gore, Nathan Gover, Beth Graue, Maxine Greene, Ove Haugalokken, Allen Hunter, David Hursh, Didacus Jules, Joyce King, Gloria Ladson-Billings, James Ladwig, Rigoberto Lasso, Regina Leite Garcia, Alan Lockwood, Allan Luke, Carmen Luke, Cameron McCarthy, Peter McLaren, Sue Middleton, Akio Nagao, Michael Olneck, Paige Porter, Fazal Rizvi, Cathy Robinson, Thomas Romberg, Judyth Sachs, Walter Secada, Tomaz Tadeu da Silva, Graham Smith, Linda Smith, Richard Smith, William Tate, Kenneth Teitelbaum, Alfred Oftedal Telhaug, Jurjo Torres Santome, Lois Weis, Yuji Yamamoto, Anna Zantiotis, and Kenneth Zeichner.

In this book in particular, I owe a very real debt to a few colleagues who never let friendship and love stand in the way of teaching me important things about my arguments: Rima Apple, James Beane, Steven Selden, Carlos Alberto Torres, and Geoff Whitty.

As with my other books, I need to acknowledge the assistance of all of the many members of the Friday Seminar at the University of Wisconsin, Madison. The past and current doctoral students and friends who have constituted that group continue to make certain that I take seriously the need to be politically and intellectually open.

Jessica Trubek did important library work for Chapter 2. Christopher Zenk served as project assistant for portions of this book and as co-author of Chapter 4. His hard work and insights were crucial to the completion of this volume, as were the efforts of Diane Falkner, the secretary with whom I work. Given the problems that sometimes arise with my arthritic joints, this book probably would not even exist without her. Carole Saltz and Carol Chambers Collins of Teachers College Press provided me with a lovely combination of friendship and editorial excellence. Their help is also very much appreciated.

Anita Oliver, a professor at La Sierra University and my co-author for Chapter 3, did the research that stimulated me to look at rightist social movements in education as being constantly in formation. Her insights and research were more than a little significant in this project.

Finally, this book is dedicated to my father, Harry Apple—printer, teacher, and political activist. Whenever we get together, political debates rage. Of course, now is no different than any time in the past. In fact, among my fondest memories is sitting with my parents—political activists both—and from as far back as I can remember, being expected to make my own positions on issues of social importance known, and having them taken seriously enough to argue about. Now that my father and I are both a bit older, the liveliness has not lessened. Nor has his—and my—commitment to struggling to build a less exploitative society. Occasionally, I get a feeling that my mother, Mimi, who died more than a decade ago and was so much a part of those intense conversations, is listening in, pleased that the Apple tradition goes on. Anyone who has had the "pleasure" of being around the political and educational discussions between me and my two now grown sons, Peter and Paul, would recognize the continuity (and perhaps might want some ear plugs as well). It's Harry's and Mimi's fault. And I'm pleased that it continues.

# Cultural Politics and Education

# CHAPTER 1

# *Education, Identity, and Cheap French Fries*

The sun glared off of the hood of the small car as we made our way along the two-lane road. The heat and humidity made me wonder if I'd have any liquid left in my body at the end of the trip and led me to appreciate Wisconsin winters a bit more. The idea of winter seemed more than a little remote in this Asian country, for which I have a good deal of fondness. But the topic at hand was not the weather; rather, it was the struggles of educators and social activists to build an education that was considerably more democratic than what was in place in that country now. This was a dangerous topic. Discussing it in philosophical and formalistically academic terms was tolerated there. Openly calling for it, and situating it within a serious analysis of the economic, political, and military power structures that now exerted control over so much of this nation's daily life, was another matter.

As we traveled along that rural road in the midst of one of the best conversations I had engaged in about the possibilities of educational transformations and the realities of the oppressive conditions so many people were facing in that land, my gaze was drawn to the side of the road. In one of those nearly accidental happenings that clarify and crystallize what reality is *really* like, my gaze fell upon a seemingly inconsequential object. At regular intervals, there were small signs planted in the dirt a few yards from where the road met the fields. The signs were more than a little familiar. They bore the insignia of one of the most famous fast food restaurants in the United States. We drove for miles past seemingly deserted fields along a flat hot plain, passing sign after sign, each a replica of the previous one, each less than a foot high. These were not billboards. Such things hardly existed in this poor rural region. Rather, they looked exactly— exactly—like the small signs one finds next to farms in the American

*1*

midwest that identify the kinds of seed corn that each farmer has planted in her or his fields. This was a good guess, it turned out.

I asked the driver—a close friend and former student of mine who had returned to this country to work for the social and educational reforms that were so necessary—what turned out to be a naive but ultimately crucial question in my own education: "Why are those signs for——there? Is there a——restaurant nearby?" My friend looked at me in amazement. "Michael, don't you know what these signs signify? There's no Western restaurant within 50 miles of where we are. These signs represent exactly what is wrong with education in this nation. Listen to this." And I listened.

The story is one that has left an indelible mark on me, for it condenses in one powerful set of historical experiences the connections between our struggles as educators and activists in so many countries and the ways differential power works in ordinary life. I cannot match the tensions and passions in my friend's voice as this story was told; nor can I convey exactly the almost eerie feelings one gets when looking at that vast, sometimes beautiful, sometimes scarred, and increasingly depopulated plain.

Yet the story is crucial to hear. Listen to this.

The government of the nation has decided that the importation of foreign capital is critical to its own survival. Bringing in American, German, British, Japanese, and other investors and factories ostensibly will create jobs, create capital for investment, and enable the nation to speed into the twenty-first century. (This is, of course, elite group talk, but let us assume that all of this indeed is truly believed by dominant groups.) One of the ways the military-dominated government has planned to do this is to focus part of its recruitment efforts on agribusiness. In pursuit of this aim, it has offered vast tracts of land to international agribusiness concerns at very low cost. The plain we are driving through is one example: Much of this land has been given over to a supplier for a large American fast food restaurant corporation, for the growing of potatoes for the restaurant's french fries, one of the trademarks of its extensive success throughout the world.

The corporation eagerly jumped at the opportunity to shift a good deal of its potato production from the United States to Asia. Since many of the farm workers in the United States were now unionized and were (correctly) asking for a livable wage, and since the government of that Asian nation officially frowned on unions of any kind, the cost of growing potatoes would be lower. Further, the land on that plain was perfect for the use of newly developed technology to plant and harvest the crop with considerably fewer workers. Machines would replace living human beings. Finally, the government was much less concerned about environmental regulations. All in all, this was a fine bargain for capital.

Of course, *people* lived on some of this land and farmed it for their own food and to sell what might be left over after their own—relatively minimal—needs were met. This deterred neither agribusiness nor the government. After all, people could be moved to make way for "progress." And after all, the villagers along that plain did not actually have deeds to the land. (They had lived there for perhaps hundreds of years, well before the invention of banks, and mortgages, and deeds—no paper, no ownership.) It would not be too hard to move the people to other areas to "free" the plain for intensive potato production and to "create jobs" by taking away the livelihood of thousands upon thousands of small-scale farmers in the region.

I listened with rapt attention as the rest of the story unfolded and as we passed by the fields with their miniature corporate signs and the abandoned villages. The people whose land had been taken for so little moved, of course. As in so many other similar places throughout what dominant groups call the Third World, they trekked to the city. They took their meager possessions and moved into the ever expanding slums within and surrounding the one place that held out some hope of finding enough paid work (if *everyone*—including children—labored) so that they could survive.

The government and major segments of the business elite officially discouraged this, sometimes by hiring thugs to burn the shanty towns, other times by keeping conditions so horrible that no one would "want" to live there. But still the dispossessed came, by the tens of thousands. Poor people are not irrational, after all. The loss of arable land had to be compensated for somehow and if it took cramming into places that were deadly at times, well what were the other choices? There *were* factories being built in and around the cities that paid incredibly low wages—sometimes less than enough money to buy sufficient food to replace the calories expended by workers in the production process—but at least there might be paid work, if one was lucky.

So the giant machines harvested the potatoes and the people poured into the cities and international capital was happy. It's not a nice story, but what does it have to do with *education*? My friend continued my education.

The military-dominated government had given all of these large international businesses 20 years of tax breaks to sweeten the conditions for their coming to that country. Thus, there was now very little money to supply the health care facilities, housing, running water, electricity, sewage disposal, and schools for the thousands upon thousands of people who had sought their future in or literally had been driven into the city. The mechanism for *not* building these necessities was quite clever. The lack of any formal educational institutions is a case in point. In order for the government to build schools it had to be shown that there was a "legitimate" need for such expenditure. Statistics had to be produced in a form that was *officially* accepted. This could be done only through the official determination of numbers of registered births. Yet, the very process of registration made it impossible for the existence of thousands of children to be recognized.

In order to register a child for school, a parent had to register the birth of the child at the local hospital or government office—few of which existed in these slum areas. Even if they could somehow find such an office, the government officially discouraged people who originally came from outside the region of the city from moving there, often refusing to recognize the legitimacy of the move. This was a way of keeping displaced farmers from coming into urban areas and thereby increasing the population. Births from people who had no "legitimate" right to be there did not count as births at all. It is a brilliant strategy through which the state creates categories of legitimacy that define social problems in quite interesting ways.[1] Foucault would have been proud, I am certain.

Thus, there are no schools, no teachers, no hospitals, no infrastructure. The root causes of this situation are not to be found in the immediate situation. They can be uncovered only if we focus on the chain of capital formation internationally and nationally, on the contradictory needs of the state, on the class relations and the relations between country and city that organize and disorganize that country.

My friend and I had been driving for quite a while now. I had forgotten about the heat. The ending sentence of the story pulled no punches. It was said slowly and quietly, in a way that made it even more compelling: "Michael, these fields are the reason there're no schools in my city. There're no schools because so many folks like cheap french fries."

I tell this story for a number of reasons. First, it is simply one of the most powerful ways I know of reminding myself and all of us of the utter importance of seeing schooling relationally, of seeing it as connected—fundamentally—to the relations of domination and exploitation (and to struggles against them) of the larger society. Second, and equally important, I tell this story to make a crucial theoretical and political point. Relations of power are indeed complex and we do need to take very seriously the postmodern focus on the local and on the multiplicity of the forms of struggle that need to be engaged in. It *is* important as well to recognize the changes that are occurring in many societies and to see the complexity of the "power/knowledge" nexus. Yet in our attempts to avoid the dangers that accompanied some aspects of previous "grand narratives," let us *not* act as if capitalism has somehow disappeared. Let us not act as if class relations don't count. Let us not act as if all of the things we learned about how the world might be understood politically have been somehow overthrown because our theories are now more complex.

The denial of basic human rights, the destruction of the environment, the deadly conditions under which people (barely) survive, the lack of a meaningful future for the thousands of children I noted in my story—all of this is not only or even primarily a "text" to be deciphered in our academic volumes as we pursue our postmodern themes. It is a reality that millions of people experience in their very bodies every day. Educational work that is not connected deeply to a powerful understanding of these realities (and this understanding cannot evacuate a serious analysis of political economy and class relations without losing much of its power) is in danger of losing its soul. The lives of our children demand no less.

## "THEY" ARE NOT LIKE "US"

The relationship between education and larger issues of economy and politics, of course, is not limited to the nation in which those potatoes for cheap french fries are grown. It is very visible here. In fact, the most powerful economic and political groups in the United States and similar nations have made it abundantly clear that for them a good education is only one that is directly tied to economic needs (but, of course, only as these needs are defined by the powerful). As I show elsewhere[2] and as I shall demonstrate later on in this book, this is quite a complex process, one filled with contradictory tendencies and impulses. Yet, much of its basic outline and history can be told readily enough by focusing on the politics of the current conservative restoration.

Many of the rightist policies now taking center stage in education and nearly everything else embody a tension between a neoliberal

emphasis on "market values" on the one hand and a neoconservative attachment to "traditional values" on the other.[3] From the former perspective, the state must be minimized, preferably by setting
private enterprise loose just as it was in the production of cheap
french fries; from the latter, the state needs to be strong in teaching
*correct* knowledge, norms, and values. From both, this society is falling apart, in part because schools don't do either of these. They are
too state-controlled and they don't mandate the teaching of what
they are "supposed" to teach. It's a bit contradictory, but as we
shall see later on, the rightist agenda has ways of dealing with such
contradictions and has managed to creatively stitch together an alliance that unites (sometimes rather tensely) its various movements.

This new hegemonic alliance has a wide umbrella. It combines
four major groups: (1) dominant economic and political elites intent
on "modernizing" the economy and the institutions connected to it;
(2) largely white working class and middle class groups who mistrust
the state and are concerned with security, the family, and traditional
knowledge and values and who form an increasingly active segment
of what might be called "authoritarian populists"; (3) economic and
cultural conservatives such as William Bennett who want a return to
"high standards," discipline, and social Darwinist competition; and
(4) a fraction of the new middle class who may not totally agree
with these other groups, but whose own professional interests and
advancement depend on the expanded use of accountability, efficiency, and management procedures that are their own cultural capital.[4]

The sphere of education is one in which the Right has been
ascendant. The social democratic goal of expanding equality of opportunity (itself a rather limited reform) has lost much of its political
potency and its ability to mobilize people. The "panic" over falling
standards, dropouts, and illiteracy; the fear of violence in schools;
the concern over the destruction of family values and religiosity, all
have had an effect. These fears are exacerbated, and used, by dominant groups within politics and the economy who have been able to
shift the debate on education (and all things social) onto their own
terrain—the terrain of traditionalism, standardization, productivity,
marketization, and industrial needs. Because so many parents *are*
justifiably concerned about the economic and cultural futures of their
children—in an economy that is increasingly conditioned by lower
wages, capital flight, and insecurity—rightist discourse connects with
the experiences of many working class and middle class people.[5]

Behind much of the conservative restoration is a clear sense of loss of control over a number of things: economic and personal security, the knowledge and values that should be passed on to children, what counts as sacred texts and authority, and relations of gender and age in the family. The binary opposition of we/they becomes important here. "We" are law abiding, "hard working, decent, virtuous, and homogeneous." The "theys" are very different. They are "lazy, immoral, permissive, and heterogeneous."[6] These binary oppositions distance most people of color, women (i.e., "feminists"), gays and lesbians, and others from the community of worthy individuals. The subjects of discrimination are now no longer those groups who have been historically oppressed, but are instead the "real Americans" who embody the idealized virtues of a romanticized past. The "theys" are undeserving. They are getting something for nothing. Policies supporting them are "sapping our way of life" and most of our economic resources, and creating government control of our lives.[7]

As with much of the ideological agenda behind such criticisms, the issues in education are not only the removal of schools from state and bureaucratic control, the enhancement of privatization and marketization, and the reconstruction of a people's character based largely on individual entrepreneurial values or on fundamentalist interpretations of "Christian morality." Behind them as well is a thoroughgoing attack on teachers and especially teacher unions. De-unionization, or at least a massive weakening of teachers' power, plays a large part here.[8]

Often what is happening is "management by stress."[9] I know of few teachers who are not feeling under attack right now, and fewer still who don't believe that this society is using its schools and government employees in general as scapegoats for larger social problems it is clearly unwilling to face.

Although my tone may be negative when discussing these seemingly unremitting attacks on the state, on schools, and on teachers' organizations, this should not be interpreted as an assumption that everything that the government does "in the public interest" in education or anything else is always wise. Indeed, it is possible to argue that because of ideological conflicts, insufficient resources, and their own interests and internal structures, governments often are organized to generate failure. In fact, some analysts have provocatively argued that, paradoxically, one of the conditions of government expansion (a very sore point with conservatives, as many know) is that it must fail to reach its goals. Although overstating his case, Ian Hunter puts it this way. "Government thereby programs its own

failure and it does so as a condition of its ongoing and truly remarkable inventiveness."[10] Governments often have ever reaching horizons, goals, and spheres of interest (e.g., equity, equality of opportunity, and so on) that under the current distribution of power and
resources simply cannot be met. Yet, in order to maintain its own
legitimacy and the continued need for all of its offices, programs, and
personnel, the state must be seen to be striving to meet these goals
and must continually measure itself against them. Thus, "demon-
strating its own failure in this way is the means by which government
opens up new tracts of social life to bureaucratic knowledge and
intervention."[11] It should not be a surprise, then, that not all of these
forms of knowledge and intervention are necessarily in the long-term
interests of those who are the subjects of them.

This is *not* to say, as the New Right does, that what is public is
bad and what is private is good, that the very idea of government
regulation is a threat to freedom. Rather, it is to remind us of the
connections among resources, power, institutional interests, failure,
and hence, continued bureaucratization and expansion. I shall show
later on that there are elements of good sense as well as bad sense in
a number of the conservative criticisms of this when I discuss some
of the struggles by parents over the curriculum in schools in the
United States. But it is clear that this very sense of bureaucratization,
inefficiency, and expansion underpins many of the attacks on
schools.

Consider the current calls for educational reform surrounding
the ties between education and (paid) work. A large portion of current reform initiatives are justified partly by wanting to enhance the
connections between education and the wider project of "meeting
the needs of the economy." This increasingly powerful economic
critique of the educational system is grounded in a number of challenges. The system is basically anti-entrepreneurial. It is horribly
wasteful. And, at a time of severe international competition, schools
are failing to produce a labor force that is sufficiently skilled, adapt-
able, and flexible.[12] As I noted, attached to this sense of schools as
producers of "human capital" is an equally crucial cultural agenda
concerning the sets of social logics that should guide our daily conduct.

For both neoliberals and neoconservatives, the educational task
here is "not only [to] encourage members of a market economy to
think of themselves as individuals in order to maximize their own
interests." This is a crucial goal, but it goes considerably further.
People also need to be encouraged to accept that it is entirely "appro-

priate for there to be winners and losers in the system."[13] A process such as this is "wealth creating."

Part of this position on the distribution of wealth—that inequality is a good thing and more inequality is an even better thing—can be found in a quote from Keith Joseph, a former minister of education for Margaret Thatcher.

> The relief of poverty has not in the past been thought to require an equal society and it is difficult to find any necessary connection between them today. On the contrary, everything in the experience of this country since the last war has combined to demonstrate that you cannot make the poor richer by making the rich poorer. You can only make the poor richer by making everyone richer including the rich.[14]

Friedrich Hayek, one of the economic theorists relied upon by conservatives, states the case even more bluntly in an earlier statement.

> If today in the United States or Western Europe the relatively poor can have a car or a refrigerator, an airplane trip or a radio, at the cost of a reasonable part of their income, this was made possible because in the past others with larger incomes were able to spend on what was then a luxury. The path of advance is greatly eased by the fact that it has been trodden before. It is because scouts have found the goal that the road can be built for the less lucky and less energetic. . . . Even the poorest today owe their relative material well-being to the results of past inequality.[15]

Of course, these empirical claims are subject to evidence. We must indeed ask of the New Right, in the United States and Britain, as the rich got richer, did the poor get less poor?[16] As I shall show in Chapter 4, the answer to this would be nearly laughable were it not for the disastrous consequences of such redistribution of wealth upwards, for that is indeed what has happened as the lives of so many people have become increasingly insecure and even desperate.

But, again, for many neoliberals and neoconservatives, there is a major culprit here: not their economic and social policies, but the school. Fix the school and nearly everything else will follow. How do we "fix" the school? Either by ratcheting up control through national curricula and testing, or by once more letting the market enter through privatized choice plans. Yet these too are not simply neutral instruments. They are filled with hidden costs and contradictions. Jonathan Kozol puts it in his own passionate way in his response to an earlier administration's advocacy of market-based choice plans, although the same criticisms can be marshaled at all of those who are so fascinated with market "solutions" to everything.

> The White House, in advancing the agenda for a "choice" plan, rests its faith on market mechanisms. What reason have the black and very poor to lend their credence to a market system that has proved so obdurate and so resistant to their pleas at every turn? Placing the burden on the individual to break down doors in finding better education for a child is attractive to conservatives because it reaffirms their faith in individual ambition and autonomy. But to ask an individual to break down doors that we have chained and bolted in advance of his [sic] arrival is unfair. [17]

Like the neoliberal position with its romantic vision of the market, the neoconservative agenda also has its interesting contradictions. While it may seem clear that such conservatism lends its support to what is "traditional" in society, it should be just as clear that its allegiance is more than a little selective. It does not support *all* that is traditional in society. [18]

One of the distinguishing features of the neoconservative position is its vision of character. There is a clear preference for incentive systems rather than the encouragement of social altruism, [19] although the latter is sometimes mentioned in its "bag of virtues" approach to moral education. Yet, the tradition of altruism has deep roots in our nation, and its expression needs to be expanded, not contracted. Selfishness is simply another form of the possessive individualism that has been one of the more destructive parts of social policies institutionalized in nations over the past 2 decades.

When they criticize the educational system, commentators of the neoconservative persuasion often are so very concerned about the supposed lack of values found among, say, inner city children. Yet, perhaps this is not the primary place we should focus. Rather, we need to ask critical questions about the values of those groups of people—groups with considerably more power and money—who have made the political and economic decisions that segregated these communities economically and racially. In essence, rather than studying the poor, we might justifiably study the nearly "pathological detachment" of the affluent and of their allies in government and neoconservative intellectual and policy circles. [20]

Even with these variations of emphases in some of the multiple but overlapping tendencies within the conservative movement, there seems to be agreement on one thing among many of these tendencies. It is an agreement whose class, race, and gender history is certainly not innocent.

In nearly all English-speaking countries, though certainly not limited to them, the various factions of the Right have forced the relationship between the market and the common good onto the political stage. Among the most influential of these ideas have been the following: that the welfare state, and the social contract that stands behind it, has not been a "good thing" for the economy because "we" simply cannot afford it; that it has limited the exercise of free democratic choice because of entrenched, mainly professional, interests; and that it is destructive to the character of the poor because it makes "them" dependent.[21]

Nearly all of the literature supporting this position invokes an earlier "golden age" before the welfare state, when policies were economically and morally sound, when normative and institutional structures were stable, and when class, gender, and racial harmony prevailed as we moved toward "progress." The state was not needed for the common good. The debate over government's role in both creating and maintaining the common good in education and elsewhere is as old as government itself. Behind the conflict over, say, workfare and learnfare in the United States and the demand that "unworthy" people should not get "something for nothing" is a very long history. This is rooted in the "workhouse test" that played such a significant part in how the United States often has dealt with the poverty caused by economic dislocations. Earlier relief systems often were based on a conscious attempt to separate the "deserving" poor from the "undeserving" poor. They also were usually characterized by a distinct lack of shyness in blaming the poor for their fate. (You know, people flock into the cities from that potato-growing plain not because of destructive economic conditions but because there's something wrong with *them*.)

In Jane Lewis's words:

> The nineteenth century poor law, which operated in England and parts of the United States, Canada and Australia, aimed firmly to distinguish between the poor and the pauper. Claimants were offered the "workhouse test" to determine whether or not they were truly destitute, the idea being the conditions within the workhouse would be less favorable than those of the lowest paid laborer. If a claimant were prepared to accept relief on such terms, then s/he might be reckoned to be truly destitute. . . . The principle was clear enough. What the nineteenth century system of welfare provision aimed to do was effectively to segregate the pauper from the market, incarcerating him or her in a workhouse

where men were deprived of the vote (if indeed they qualified for one under the limited franchise) and where such work as was offered ([often] stone crushing for men and oakum picking for women) would not interfere with the local labor market. [22]

In essence, the poor were a "race apart." [23] They could be incarcerated, deprived of basic rights of citizenship, and treated as not worthy of personhood. The relationship of these ideas to class dynamics is clear. Yet, there has always been a connection between these policies and race and gender as well.

Take the Victorian ideal, for example, as it was institutionalized at the turn of the century in a number of nations. For Victorians, as for many of today's conservatives, social problems disappeared when the family was strong and effective. Such a family—husbands who were reliable breadwinners and wives who were efficient managers in the home—cared for the old and infirm and socialized children into "the habits of labor and obedience." [24] Women's paid work was frowned upon because it might damage male work incentives. Yet, the Victorians were of two minds when it came to poor women, especially those who were alone. While they wished to encourage and/or enforce male labor market participation and were attached to the idea that the "proper" role of women was in the home, applying the same standard to the increasingly large numbers of, say, widowed, deserted, or unmarried mothers presented a dilemma. [25] And here an intricate moral hierarchy entered to complement the effects of the even earlier losses of poor people's personhood, respect, and citizenship rights.

Government officials had a decision to make. Were these women to be treated as mothers or workers? On the whole, they chose the latter. Here the moral hierarchy entered in new forms. Widows were counted as "more deserving." They usually were allowed to keep as many children, usually one or two, as they could support through their paid labor. The rest were taken to the workhouse or to orphanages. "Deserted wives" who had the courage (and it did take immense courage) to seek help and to officially declare that they indeed were destitute were treated much more harshly. Government authorities were deeply suspicious of collusion between spouses. Working class men might be living off "their women's" benefits. "Unmarried mothers" were seen as morally reprehensible. Often the only relief available to them was entering the workhouse. [26]

All too much of this is redolent of current rightist discourse around the poor and especially poor women (and men). This constructs an image of, for example, the poor African American man who lives off "his woman's" welfare check; of morally uncontrollable poor women; of poor unmarried women who drop out of school and have baby after baby simply to get more money. This distressingly biased and empirically problematic image of the poor is what stands behind many of the social and educational policies of the conservative restoration today. The answer for the rightist coalition is to revivify their image of the traditional family, to force a form of slavery or endentured servitude on poor people of color and the poor in general, and once again to create a vision of the poor as totally the cause of their own conditions.[27] Back to the future?

While this shall be discussed in greater detail in Chapter 3, the *image* of the family (not the reality, which is and has been very varied throughout the history of the United States)[28] plays a central part in this ideological drama. Just as in earlier times, the discourse of the family can be used for many social purposes. In this case, as before, its use is more than a little retrogressive.

For example, for the neoconservative and authoritarian populist Right it is the family's role to act as a "guardian of social stability within an aggressively competitive economy." How are we to minimize the state? Part of the answer is to maximize the family.[29] In Arnot's words, "By rehabilitating the family, [we] could break down the 'scrounger state' and through a 'moral crusade' counter the effects of permissiveness and arguably feminism."[30]

It is evident from this discussion that there clearly are patriarchal elements and intentions within the conservative restoration; but what is behind a good many of its policies is not only an antifeminist stance. We need always to remember that the guiding set of principles for a significant portion of this agenda is to increase profits by raising productivity, cutting costs, weakening the collective organizations of paid workers, and disciplining workers through a fear of unemployment.[31] Given the need of capital for the paid labor of women, the Right could not pursue a policy of merely returning women to the family and domestic labor. It had to aggressively integrate women into the paid labor market. Yet, the process through which this integration occurred was carried out under the "worst possible terms" for these women.[32] Protection was reduced; unemployment rates remained high; child care was not provided by the state; domestic burdens were actually increased as the state withdrew its support of social services and programs and then threw its responsibilities onto a private sector that never totally compensated for the loss. For working class women and women of color, the cumulative

effect of these policies was devastating. Their opportunities were severely restricted and the kinds of work available to them were indeed
"under the worst possible conditions." The situation was and is
more than a little reminiscent of "cheap french fries." An understanding of gender, *and* race, *and* class is essential, then, to understand both the contradictory intentions and effects of the conservative
restoration. This will be clear throughout this book.

These intentions and effects at times appear contradictory; for
example, the proper role for women is at once to be recruited into the
paid workforce for economic reasons, *and* to stay at home in order to
reproduce the "traditional family." But, overall, the rightist alliance
effectively has created the conditions that give it increasing hegemonic power over policies and over even how we talk about what is
right and wrong in the economy, social welfare, politics, and, as
many of you know all too well from personal experience, education.
The discourse of the alliance combines two kinds of language: (1) of
children as "future workers," of privatization and market choice for
"consumers," of business needs, and of tighter accountability and
control; and (2) of "Christian" values, the Western tradition, the
traditional family, and back to "basics." These two languages, spoken simultaneously, have created such a din that it is hard to hear
anything else. Putting these two kinds of language together, as the
rightist coalition does, gives it immense power. It threatens to become truly hegemonic.

## HEGEMONIC CULTURES

In this volume, as in my others, I often employ a word found in
the last sentence of the previous paragraph: *hegemony*. It is a concept
with a long and varied history.[33] It remains one of my favorite concepts, not because of its poetics as it slips off the tongue (which it
doesn't do anyway) and not because it gives a person instant theoretical legitimacy (in some circles it makes people nervous). Rather, I
use it because of its usefulness as a tool in unpacking crucial parts of
not only the powerful economic and family agenda I just discussed,
but also of the cultural agenda of restorational politics in education. It
is an essential tool in uncovering some of the ways in which differential power is circulated and used in education and the larger society.

The concept of hegemony refers to a process in which dominant
groups in society come together to form a bloc and sustain leadership
over subordinate groups. One of the most important elements that

such an idea implies is that a power bloc does not have to rely on coercion. (Although at times it does. Think of the fact that the United States incarcerates a larger percent of its population—and especially men and women of color—than any other nation of its type in the world.) Rather, it relies on *winning consent* to the prevailing order,[34] by forming an ideological umbrella under which different groups who usually might not totally agree with each other can stand. The key to this is offering a compromise so that such groups feel as if their concerns are being listened to (hence, rhetoric is essential in this process), but without dominant groups having to give up their leadership of general social tendencies. As I argued earlier in this chapter, this is exactly what has happened in so many of our nations as rightist discourse becomes increasingly dominant in the formation of our common sense.[35] The fact that we are tacitly returning to a form of the workhouse test and to a condition of denying person rights to many of the poor—and that this is becoming widely accepted—documents my point.

It is, of course, crucial to note that in any given historical situation, hegemonic control can be found only as the *partial* exercise of leadership by dominant groups, or by an alliance of dominant groups, in some, but certainly not all, spheres of society. The most powerful forces in our societies will not be equally successful in the economy, in the law, in state-financed educational institutions, in the mass media and the arts, in religion, and in the family and civil society as a whole.[36] As Jim McGuigan states, ''The dominant culture never commands the field entirely: it must struggle continually with residual and emergent cultures.''[37] Equally important is the fact that while hegemonic relations often have been thought of in class terms— and it is of great import to continue to think of them in that way—as I noted, it is essential that we always recognize the multiplicity of relations of power surrounding race, gender, sexuality, and ''ability.''

Race—which is *not* a biological entity but a social construction— provides an example here.[38] Take the attempt by neoconservatives to have schools and the media create a single, unitary ''American identity.'' It is not imposed, in the usual sense of that word. Rather, it is put forward by an alliance of dominant groups in a way that the alliance hopes will enable all the other groups it wants under its ideological umbrella to find something in it for themselves. Yes, some of you are in very shaky economic circumstances, feel culturally or religiously marginalized, are condemned to attend what are seen to be failing schools that are racially tense and underfunded, and are feeling immensely insecure in nearly all parts of your life. Some of you live in rural and urban areas where conditions are nearly as bad as those I noted in my opening story in this chapter. But "we" are all one. We are all part of one identity, a nation of immigrants. This is hegemonic discourse at its creative "best."

Edward Said nicely points to part of the danger:

> Before we can agree on what the American identity is made of, we have to concede that as an immigrant settler society superimposed on the ruins of considerable native presence, American identity is too varied to be a unitary and homogeneous thing; indeed the battle within it is between advocates of a unitary identity and those who see the whole as a complex but not reductively unified one. [39]

Like Said, I believe that it is only the second of these perspectives that is fully sensitive to the reality of historical experiences. As he puts it, "Partly because of empire, all cultures are involved in one another, none is single and pure, all are hybrid, heterogeneous, extraordinarily differentiated, and unmonolithic." [40]

There is too much talk of such heterogeneity as somehow leading to the "Balkanization" or "Lebanonization" of the United States, as if somehow the republic will dissolve. (Arthur Schlesinger's *The Disuniting of America* is a case in point.) [41] Rather, in my mind, it seems so much better to explore our multiple historical stories rather than repress or deny them as many neoconservatives would have us do. Once again, Edward Said, one of our wisest commentators on cultural politics, states part of the argument best.

> The fact that the United States contains so many histories, many of them now clamoring for attention, is by no means to be suddenly feared since many of them were always there, and out of them an American society and politics . . . were in fact created. In other words, the result of present debates over multiculturalism is hardly to be "Lebanonization," and if these debates point the way for political changes in the way women, minorities, [gays and lesbians], and recent immigrants see themselves, then it is not to be feared or defended against. What needs to be remembered is that narratives of emancipation and enlightenment in their strongest form were also narratives of *integration* not separation, the stories of people who had been excluded from the main group but who were now fighting for a place in it. And if the old and habitual ideas of the main group were not flexible or generous enough to admit new groups, then these ideas need changing, a far better thing to do than reject the emerging groups. [42]

I said previously that in my mind Said gets much of the argument right. However, there are dangers here as well. Such an argument positions "the main group" as the ultimate arbiter, as the judge of inclusion and exclusion, when in a time of restorational politics this in itself is part of the problem and what needs to be rethought. Should, say, a largely white dominant culture have the ultimate right to judge which African American, American Indian, Latino/Latina, Asian American, or other stories of the past, present, or future are "legitimate," are the ones that are given the official imprimatur? This is a complex question, but clearly the intuitions of many of us are to say no, and correctly, I think.

Said's insights about the nature of culture and history could have been phrased a little better as well, since some of his language can be employed to support a position on multiculturalism that is more than a little powerful today, even though it is deeply flawed. It is a discourse that, while having progressive-sounding elements and avowed by some liberals, shows the hegemonic umbrella in use. Let us take as an example the vision of America's past that I mentioned a moment ago. All too many textbooks and curriculum materials in our schools construct the United States as the story of "immigrants." "We" are a nation of immigrants. "We" are *all* immigrants, from the original First Nation (Indian) people who trekked across the Bering Strait to the more recent people from, say, Eastern Europe, Latin America, Asia, and Africa. Well, sure we are. But such a story totally misconstrues the differential conditions that existed. Some immigrants came in *chains*, were slaves and faced centuries of repression and government-mandated segregation. And there is a world of difference here.

While words are not everything—and some of our political debates over "correct words" *can and do* serve as an excuse to not engage in larger issues or to stereotype in unfortunate ways the speaker of such words—words do count. They often contain an historical logic within themselves. Thus, we must be cautious in employing the discourse of a nation of immigrants so that it does not ignore the very real differences in historical experiences of identifiable, differently positioned groups of citizens. I shall have much more to say about this in my analysis of arguments for a national curriculum later on.

Thus, language does count. Take as but one example the seemingly simple word "disadvantaged." It is worth noting that the word *disadvantaged* implies that one's problems are largely the result of bad luck. In essence, there are no agents of domination. To say "op-

pressed'' rather than disadvantaged implies something more powerful. It signifies that oppressive structures exist.[43] It is exactly this
difference to which I wish to point. I do not want to lose sight of the
patterns such oppressive conditions take, at the same time as I explore the complicated ways in which power operates in cultural, political, and economic ways in this society.

## CULTURAL POLITICS AND EDUCATION

The threads that I have woven together here to form a picture of
current tendencies, and of some of their checkered pasts, contain
various elements: economic goals and values; visions of both the
family and race, gender, and class relations; the politics of culture,
difference, and identity; and the role of the state in all of this. In order
to think seriously about the cultural politics of education, none of
these elements can be ignored. The following chapters demonstrate
why this is the case and provide examples of how one might take
these varied elements seriously. Some chapters focus on the broad
cultural/ideological struggles now going on around and in schools.
Others shine the spotlight of critical analysis directly on the economy
and its connections to educational discourse, policy, and practice.
Some direct our attention to cultural politics and the creation of common sense at a national level. Others are decidedly and properly
local.

Chapter 2 examines the most significant proposals for educational ''reform'' that have come from the neoliberal and neoconservative alliance. Its major focus is on proposals for a national curriculum
and a program of national testing. Chapter 2 situates these proposals
within the overall tendencies and contradictions in this alliance and
shows how the conservative coalition creatively brings together under its leadership a variety of groups who are not always in agreement.

I argue that one of the perverse effects of a national curriculum
actually will be to ''legitimize inequality.'' It may in fact help create
the illusion that whatever the massive differences in schools, they all
have something in common.[44] They are all equal culturally. I inten-
tionally use the word *illusion* here to signify the utter power of the
very real differences that exist between, say, poor inner city and
rural schools and those of the affluent suburbs. As Jonathan Kozol so
vividly documents, the differences in resources and power, and the
attendant experiences of students, teachers, and community mem-

bers that result from these differences, are indeed "savage."[45] I also argue that the rapid movement toward centralization in curricula and testing may be an ideal first step toward one of the Right's long-term goals, privatization. In the process, I suggest that we need to think about questions of a common culture and a common curriculum in ways very different from those currently circulating.

I noted earlier in this introductory chapter that one of the reasons the conservative restoration has been able to gain adherents is the fear of an ever increasing bureaucratization and expansion of the state. One doesn't need to align oneself with rightist positions to agree that a government that doesn't listen, that assumes that it always knows more than its ordinary citizens, that establishes ways of divorcing itself from the deeply felt concerns of these citizens, is not wise. Indeed, these kinds of criticisms are part of the driving force behind so much of the democratic socialist and democratic populist agendas. Thus, although I am deeply worried about the authoritarian impulses behind a good deal of the conservative restoration—and especially of the conservative religious fundamentalist parts of this alliance—I want us to take their criticisms very seriously.

In Chapter 3, Anita Oliver and I do exactly this. We analyze the ideological positions that provide the grounding upon which fundamentalists rest their case against public schools, and argue that schools do have much to worry about, given the growing power of this movement. But the chapter goes much further. It goes inside school districts themselves, to demonstrate how the bureaucratic structures and responses of schools sometimes actually create the conditions under which right-wing movements grow and thrive. We also argue that it is at the local level that such national movements can be interrupted and contested.

Chapter 3 serves other purposes as well, however. As with the chapter on national curricula and national testing, it has a theoretical agenda. We aim to demonstrate, in concrete ways, how the usually disparate neo-Gramscian and postmodern and poststructural traditions can be put together to usefully illuminate the dynamics of power in and around education in real schools. This is a risky enterprise both conceptually and politically. Placing these traditions close together so that they rub and bump against each other in creative ways, may, as I hope to show, enable us to see important things about educational policy and practice that we might otherwise miss. Yet, a considerable number of individuals within universities have built careers upon "dissing." They go to great lengths to distance "the new" from the "old" and/or make increasingly arid metatheoretical distinctions between and within these varied traditions. In my mind, however, theories count depending on the *work* they enable us to do. In Pierre Bourdieu's apposite words, "trespassing is a prerequisite to advance."[46] And if continuing to trespass back and forth over the borders between "neo" and "post" does indeed enable us to do crucial analytic/empirical/political/educational work, then that's just fine with me. I'll leave the border policing to others. I'm less interested in arcane academic distinctions or the mobility politics within the academy that make such distinctions "important," than I am in understanding the limits and possibilities of critical actions surrounding cultural politics and education.

While segments of the hegemonic alliance want to evacuate difference by positing *their* sense of an American identity or by constructing a common culture that washes crucial historical differences and experiences away, other elements within this coalition are much less interested in these cultural battles, except where it helps them bring the conservative religious fundamentalists under the umbrella of their leadership. For them, as for the all too common stereotype of old-style Marxists, "It's the economy, stupid." Our problems will be solved if we reorganize all of our institutions around *their* sense of economic needs. Education here becomes a product like bread or cars, and the only culture worth talking about is "enterprise culture" and the flexible skills, knowledge, dispositions, and values needed for economic competition.[47]

One of the primary justifications for the attack on public schools, as I noted, is the nature of the economy. "Our" economy is hampered in its competitive potential due to low standards, a lack of work discipline, and poor achievement. The construction of the school dropout and the "at risk" student as the metaphor for the major problem of our lack of economic competitiveness is an archetypical example of how dominant groups export the blame from the economy onto the schools. By using the issue of dropouts as a lever to pry lose the connections between schooling and the economy, Chapter 4 examines the social construction of dropping out as a problem and situates it directly into what the current and future economy actually looks like. The real economy, as opposed to the rosy picture of steady economic recovery that benefits everyone, may give us cause for alarm not only now but in terms of the future prospects of millions of our children.

With this in mind, in Chapter 4 we also shall hear the words of a number of students who—after having stayed in school rather than dropping out—are now experiencing what life is like in so many of the jobs now available in that supposedly rosy economy. These voices provide eloquent testimony about the lives to which we are condemning so many of our youth if we accept dominant definitions of this society's problems and solutions.

I do not mean the last sentence of the previous paragraph to be merely rhetorical. The terms that are used to describe social and educational life are also active forces in shaping it. One of the most crucial aspects of politics is the struggle to define social reality and to interpret people's inchoate aspirations and needs.[48] Cultural politics in education is not only about the complex issues of what and whose cultural capital becomes official knowledge. Nor is it only about whose visions of the family, the government, identity, and the economy are to be realized in our institutions and in our daily life. All of these *are* of great importance, of course. However, cultural politics is also, and profoundly, about the resources we employ to challenge existing relations, to defend those counterhegemonic forms that now exist, or to bring new forms into existence. As I note in my concluding chapter, this is part of a conscious collective attempt to *name the world differently*, to positively refuse to accept dominant meanings, and to positively assert the possibility that it could be different. Speaking only partly metaphorically, we might say that it represents our continuing attempt to live without cheap french fries.

# CHAPTER 2

# The Politics of Official Knowledge: Does a National Curriculum Make Sense?

Education is deeply implicated in the politics of culture. The curriculum is never simply a neutral assemblage of knowledge, somehow appearing in the texts and classrooms of a nation. It is always part of a *selective tradition*, someone's selection, some group's vision of legitimate knowledge. It is produced out of the cultural, political, and economic conflicts, tensions, and compromises that organize and disorganize a people. As I argue in *Ideology and Curriculum* and *Official Knowledge*, the decision to define some groups' knowledge as the most legitimate, as official knowledge, while other groups' knowledge hardly sees the light of day, says something extremely important about who has power in society.[1]

Think of social studies texts that continue to speak of "the Dark Ages" rather than the historically more accurate and much less racist phrase, "the age of African and Asian Ascendancy" or books that treat Rosa Parks as merely a naive African American woman who was simply too tired to go to the back of the bus, rather than discussing her training in organized civil disobedience at the Highlander Folk School. The realization that teaching, especially at the elementary school level, has in large part been defined as women's paid work—with its accompanying struggles over autonomy, pay, respect, and deskilling—documents the connections between curriculum and teaching and the history of gender politics as well.[2] Thus, whether we like it or not, differential power intrudes into the very heart of curriculum, teaching, and evaluation. What *counts* as knowledge, the ways in which it is organized, who is empowered to teach it, what counts as an appropriate display of having learned it, and—just as critically—who is allowed to ask and answer all these questions, are part and parcel of how dominance and subordination are reproduced

22

and altered in this society.[3] There is, then, always a *politics* of official knowledge, a politics that embodies conflict over what some regard as simply neutral descriptions of the world and what others regard as elite conceptions that empower some groups while disempowering others.

Speaking in general about how elite culture, habits, and "tastes" function, Pierre Bourdieu puts it this way:

> The denial of lower, coarse, vulgar, venal, servile—in a word, natural—enjoyment, which constitutes the sacred sphere of culture, implies an affirmation of the superiority of those who can be satisfied with the sublimated, refined, disinterested, gratuitous, distinguished pleasures forever closed to the profane. That is why art and cultural consumption are predisposed, consciously and deliberatively or not, to fulfill a social function of legitimating social difference.[4]

As he goes on to say, these cultural forms, "through the economic and social conditions which they presuppose, . . . are bound up with the systems of dispositions (habitus) characteristic of different classes and class fractions."[5] Thus, cultural form and content function as markers of class.[6] The granting of sole legitimacy to such a system of culture through its incorporation within the official centralized curriculum, then, creates a situation in which the markers of "taste" become the markers of people. The school becomes a class school.

The tradition of scholarship and activism that has formed me has been based on exactly these insights: the complex relationships between economic capital and cultural capital, the role of the school in reproducing and challenging the multitude of unequal relations of power (ones that go well beyond class, of course), and the ways the content and organization of the curriculum, pedagogy, and evaluation function in all of this.

It is at exactly this time that these issues must be taken most seriously. This is a period—what I called the *conservative restoration*—when the conflicts over the politics of official knowledge are severe. At stake I believe is the very idea of public education, and the very idea of a curriculum that responds to the cultures and histories of large and growing segments of the American population. Even with a "moderate" Democratic presidential administration temporarily in Washington at the time of this writing, many of its own commitments embody the tendencies I shall speak of here. In fact, it is exactly *because* there is now a somewhat more "moderate" administration at a national level that we must think quite carefully about what can happen in the future as it is pulled—for political reasons—in increasingly conservative directions due to its own weak commitments and the growing power of rightist politicians in Congress and at the state and local levels.

I want to instantiate these arguments through an analysis of the proposals for a national curriculum and national testing. But in order to understand them, we must think *relationally*, we must connect these proposals to the larger program of the conservative restoration. I want to argue that behind the educational justifications for a national curriculum and national testing is an ideological attack that is very dangerous. Its effects will be truly damaging to those who already have the most to lose in this society. I shall first present a few interpretive cautions. Then I shall analyze the general project of the rightist agenda. Third, I shall show the connections between national curricula and national testing and the increasing focus on privatization and "choice" plans. And, finally, I want to discuss the patterns of differential benefits that will likely result from all this.


## THE QUESTION OF A NATIONAL CURRICULUM

Where should those of us who count ourselves a part of the long progressive tradition in education stand in relationship to the call for a national curriculum?

At the outset, I want to make something clear. I am not opposed in principle to a national curriculum. Nor am I opposed in principle to the idea or activity of testing. Rather, I want to provide a more conjunctural set of arguments, one based on a claim that at this time— given the balance of social forces—there are very real dangers of which we must be quite conscious. I shall confine myself largely to the negative case in this chapter. My task is a simple one: to raise enough serious questions to make us stop and think about the implications of moving in this direction in a time of conservative triumphalism.

We are not the only nation where a largely rightist coalition has put such proposals on the educational agenda. In England, a national curriculum, first introduced by the Thatcher government, is now mostly in place. It consists of "core and foundation subjects" such as mathematics, science, technology, history, art, music, physical education, and a modern foreign language. Working groups to determine standard goals, "attainment targets," and content in each have already brought forth their results. This is accompanied by a national system of achievement testing—one that is both expensive and takes a considerable amount of classroom time—for all students in state-run schools at the ages of 7, 11, 14, and 16.[7]

The assumption in many quarters is that we must follow the lead of other nations—such as Britain and especially Japan—or we shall be left behind. Yet, it is crucial that we understand that we *already* have a national curriculum, but that it is determined by the complicated nexus of state textbook adoption policies and the market in textbook publishing.[8] Thus, we have to ask if a national curriculum—one that undoubtedly will be linked to a system of national goals and nationally standardized instruments of evaluation (quite probably standardized tests, due to time and money)—is *better* than an equally widespread but somewhat more hidden national curriculum established by state textbook adoption states (such as California and Texas with their control of 20–30% of the market in textbooks).[9] Despite the existence of this hidden national curriculum, there is a growing feeling that a standardized set of national curricular goals and guidelines is essential to "raise standards" and to hold schools accountable for their students' achievement or lack of it.

It is true that many people from an array of educational and political positions are involved in calls for higher standards, more rigorous curricula at a national level, and a system of national testing. Yet we must always ask one question: What group is leading these "reform" efforts? This, of course, leads to another, broader question. Who will benefit and who will lose as a result of all this? I shall contend that, unfortunately, rightist groups are indeed setting the political agenda in education and that, in general, the same pattern of benefits that has characterized nearly all areas of social policy—in which the top 20% of the population reap 80% of the benefits[10]—will be reproduced here.

Of course, we need to be very cautious of the genetic fallacy, the assumption that *because* a policy or a practice originates within a distasteful position it is fundamentally determined, in all its aspects, by its origination within that tradition. Take Edward L. Thorndike, one of the most influential educational psychologists of the early twentieth century. The fact that his social beliefs were often repugnant—with his participation in the popular eugenics movement and his notions of racial, gender, and class hierarchies—does not necessarily destroy, at each and every movement, his research on learning. While I am not at all a supporter of this paradigm of research—whose epistemological and social implications continue to need major criticism[11]—to oppose it requires a different kind of argument than that based on origination. (Indeed, one can find some progressive educators in the past who turned to Thorndike for support for some of their claims about what needed to be transformed in our curriculum and pedagogy.)

Of course, it is not only those who are identified with the rightist project who argue for a national curriculum. Others who historically have been identified with a more liberal agenda have attempted to make a case.[12] Smith, O'Day, and Cohen suggest a positive if cautionary vision for a national curriculum. A national curriculum would involve the invention of new examinations—a technically, conceptually, and politically difficult task. It would require the teaching of more rigorous content and thus would ask teachers to engage in more demanding and exciting work. Our teachers and administrators would have to "deepen their knowledge of academic subjects and change their conceptions of knowledge itself." Teaching and learning would have to be seen as "more active and inventive." Teachers, administrators, and students would need "to become more thoughtful, collaborative, and participatory."[13]

In Smith, O'Day, and Cohen's words:

> Conversion to a national curriculum could only succeed if the work of conversion were conceived and undertaken as a grand, cooperative learning venture. Such an enterprise would fail miserably if it were conceived and organized chiefly as a technical process of developing new exams and materials and then "disseminating" or implementing them.[14]

They go on to say:

> A worthwhile, effective national curriculum would also require the creation of much new social and intellectual connective tissue. For instance, the content and pedagogy of teacher education would have to be closely related to the content of and pedagogy of the schools' curriculum. The content and pedagogy of examinations would have to be tied to those of the curriculum and teacher education. Such connections do not now exist.[15]

The authors conclude that such a revitalized system, one in which such coordination would be built, "will not be easy, quick, or cheap," especially if it is to preserve variety and initiative. "If Americans continue to want educational reform on the cheap, a national curriculum would be a mistake."[16] I couldn't agree more with this last point.

Yet, what they do not sufficiently recognize is that much of what they fear is already going on in the very linkage for which they call. Even more important, it is what they do not pay sufficient attention to—the connections between a national curriculum and national testing and the larger rightist agenda—that constitutes the greatest danger. I wish to focus on this.

### BETWEEN NEOCONSERVATIVISM AND NEOLIBERALISM

Conservatism by its very name announces one interpretation of its agenda. It conserves. Other interpretations are possible, of course. One could say, somewhat more wryly, that conservatism believes that nothing should be done for the first time.[17] Yet in many ways, this would be deceptive. For with the Right now in ascendancy in many nations, we are witnessing a much more activist project. Conservative politics now are very much the politics of alteration; clearly the idea of "Do nothing for the first time" is not a sufficient explanation of what is going on either in education or elsewhere.[18]

Conservatism has in fact meant different things at different times and places. At times, it involves defensive actions; at other times, it involves taking initiative against the status quo.[19] Today we are witnessing both.

Because of this, it is important that I set out the larger social context in which the current politics of official knowledge operates. There has been a breakdown in the accord that guided a good deal of educational policy since World War II. Powerful groups within government and the economy, and within "authoritarian populist"[20] social movements, have been able to redefine—often in very retrogressive ways—the terms of debate in education, social welfare, and other areas of the common good. What education is *for* is being transformed. No longer is education seen as part of a social alliance in which many "minority"[21] groups, women, teachers, community activists, progressive legislators and government officials, and others joined together to propose (limited) social democratic policies for schools: expanding educational opportunities, attempts at equalizing outcomes, developing special programs in bilingual and multicultural education, and so on. As I noted in Chapter 1, a new alliance has been formed, one that has increasing power in educational and social policy. This power bloc combines business with the New Right and with neoconservative intellectuals. Its interests are not in increasing the life chances of women, people of color, or labor. Rather it aims at providing the educational conditions believed necessary both for increasing international competitiveness, profit, and discipline and for returning us to a romanticized past of the "ideal" home, family, and school.[22]

The power of this alliance can be seen in a number of educational policies and proposals: (1) programs for "choice" such as voucher plans and tax credits to make schools more like the thoroughly idealized free-market economy; (2) the movement at national and state levels throughout the country to "raise standards" and mandate both teacher and student "competencies" and basic curricular goals and knowledge increasingly through the implementation of statewide and national testing; (3) the increasingly effective attacks on the school curriculum for its anti-family and anti-free-enterprise "bias," its secular humanism, its lack of patriotism, and its supposed neglect of the knowledge and values of the "Western tradition" and of "real knowledge"; and (4) the growing pressure to make the perceived needs of business and industry into the primary goals of the school.[23]

In essence, the new alliance in favor of the conservative restoration has integrated education into a wider set of ideological commitments. The alliance's objectives in education are the same as those that guide its economic and social welfare goals. These include the expansion of the "free market," the drastic reduction of government responsibility for social needs (although the Clinton administration originally did mediate this in symbolic and not very extensive—or very expensive—ways), the reinforcement of intensely competitive structures of mobility, the lowering of people's expectations for economic security, and the popularization of what is clearly a form of social Darwinist thinking.[24]

As I have argued at length elsewhere, the political Right in the United States has been very successful in mobilizing support *against* the educational system and its employees, often exporting the crisis in the economy to the schools. Thus, one of its major achievements has been to shift the blame for unemployment and underemployment, for the loss of economic competitiveness, and for the supposed breakdown of "traditional" values and standards in the family, education, and paid and unpaid workplaces, *from* the economic, cultural, and social policies and effects of dominant groups *to* the school and other public agencies. As I stated in Chapter 1, "public" now is the center of all evil; "private" is the center of all that is good.[25]

Four trends have characterized the conservative restoration in both the United States and Britain—privatization, centralization, vo-cationalization, and differentiation. [26] These are actually the results largely of differences within the most powerful wings of this alliance—neoliberalism and neoconservatism—to which I pointed earlier.

Neoliberalism has a vision of the weak state. A society that lets the "invisible hand" of the free market guide *all* aspects of its forms of social interaction is seen as both efficient and democratic. On the other hand, neoconservatism is guided by a vision of the strong state in certain areas, especially over the politics of the body and gender and race relations, over standards, values, and conduct, and over what knowledge should be passed on to future generations. [27] Those two positions do not easily sit side by side in the conservative coalition.

Thus, the rightist movement is contradictory. Is there not something paradoxical about linking all of the feelings of loss and nostalgia to the unpredictability of the market, "in replacing loss by sheer flux"? [28] The contradictions between neoconservative and neoliberal elements in the rightist coalition are "solved" through a policy of what Roger Dale has called *conservative modernization.* [29] Such a policy is engaged in

> simultaneously "freeing" individuals for economic purposes while controlling them for social purposes; indeed, in so far as economic "freedom" increases inequalities, it is likely to increase the need for social control. A "small, strong state" limits the range of its activities by transferring to the market, which it defends and legitimizes, as much welfare [and other activities] as possible. In education, the new reliance on competition and choice is not all pervasive; instead, "what is intended is a dual system, polarized between . . . market schools and minimum schools". [30]

That is, there will be a relatively less regulated and increasingly privatized sector for the children of the better off. For the rest—and the economic status and racial composition of the people in, say, our urban areas who attend these minimum schools will be thoroughly predictable—the schools will be tightly controlled and policed, and will continue to be underfunded and unlinked to decent paid employment.

One of the major effects of the combination of marketization and strong state is "to remove educational policies from public debate." That is, the choice is left up to individual parents and "the hidden hand of unintended consequences does the rest." In the process, the very idea of education being part of a *public* political sphere in which its means and ends are publicly debated atrophies. [31]

There are major differences between democratic attempts at enhancing people's rights over the policies and practices of schooling and the neoliberal emphasis on marketization and privatization. The goal of the former is to *extend politics*, to "revivify democratic practice by devising ways of enhancing public discussion, debate, and negotiation." The former is inherently based on a vision of democracy that is seen as an educative practice. The latter, on the other hand, seeks to *contain politics*. It wants to *reduce all politics to economics*, to an ethic of "choice" and "consumption." [32] The world, in essence, becomes a vast supermarket.

Enlarging the private sector so that buying and selling—in a word, competition—is the dominant ethic of society involves a set of closely related propositions. It assumes that more individuals are motivated to work harder under these conditions. After all, we "already know" that public servants are inefficient and slothful, while private enterprises are efficient and energetic. It assumes that self-interest and competitiveness are the engines of creativity. More knowledge, more experimentation, is created and used to alter what we have now. In the process, less waste is created. Supply and demand stay in a kind of equilibrium. A more efficient machine is thus created, one that minimizes administrative costs and ultimately distributes resources more widely. [33]

This is, of course, not meant simply to privilege the few. However, it is the equivalent of saying that everyone has the right to climb the north face of the Eiger or scale Mount Everest without exception, providing, of course, that one is very good at mountain climbing and has the institutional and financial resources to do it. [34]

Thus, in a conservative society, access to a society's private resources (and, remember, the attempt is to make nearly *all* of society's resources private) is dependent largely on one's ability to pay. And this is dependent on one's being a person of an *entrepreneurial or efficiently acquisitive class type*. On the other hand, access to society's public resources (that rapidly decreasing segment) is dependent on need. [35] In a conservative society, the former is to be maximized, the latter is to be minimized.

However, the conservatism of the conservative alliance does not merely depend, for a large portion of its arguments and policies, on a particular view of human nature—a view of human nature as primarily self-interested. It has gone further; it has set out to degrade that human nature, to force all people to conform to what at first could only pretend to be true. Unfortunately, it has succeeded in no small measure. Perhaps blinded by their own absolutist and reductive vision of what it means to be human, many of our political "leaders" do not seem to be capable of recognizing what they have done. They have set out, aggressively, to drag down the character of a people,[36] while at the same time attacking the poor and the disenfranchised for their supposed lack of values and character.

Some of my anger begins to show here. You will forgive me, I trust; but if we cannot get angry about the lives of our children, what can we be angry about?

### CURRICULUM, TESTING, AND A COMMON CULTURE

As Whitty reminds us, what is striking about the rightist coalition's policies is its capacity to connect the emphasis on traditional knowledge and values, authority, standards, and national identity of the neoconservatives and authoritarian populists with the emphasis on the extension of market-driven principles into all areas of our society, as advocated by the neoliberals.[37] Thus, a national curriculum—coupled with rigorous national standards and a system of testing that is performance driven—is able at one and the same time to be aimed at "modernization" of the curriculum and the efficient "production" of better "human capital" *and* to represent a nostalgic yearning for a romanticized past.[38] When tied to a program of market-driven policies such as voucher and choice plans, such a national system of standards, testing, and curricula—while perhaps internally inconsistent—is an ideal compromise within the rightist coalition.

But one could still ask, Won't a national curriculum coupled with a system of national achievement testing contradict in practice the concomitant emphasis on privatization and school choice? Can one really do both simultaneously? I want to claim here that this apparent contradiction may not be as substantial as it appears. Transferring power from the local level to the center is not necessarily a long-term aim of powerful elements within the conservative coalition, although for some neoconservatives who favor a strong state when it comes to morality, values, and standards this may indeed be the case. Rather, those powerful elements would prefer to decenter such power altogether and redistribute it according to market forces and thus tacitly disempower those who already have less power, while using a rhetoric of empowering the "consumer." In part, both a national curriculum and national testing can be seen as "necessary concessions in pursuit of this long term aim."[39]

In a time of a loss of government legitimacy and a crisis in educational authority relations, the government must be seen to be doing something about raising educational standards. After all, this is exactly what it promises to offer to "consumers" of education. A national curriculum is crucial here. Its major value does not lie in its supposed encouragement of standardized goals and content and of levels of achievement in what are considered the most important subject areas: a goal that should not be totally dismissed. Instead, the major role of a national curriculum is in *providing the framework within which national testing can function*. It enables the establishment of a procedure that supposedly can give consumers "quality tags" on schools so that "free market forces" can operate to the fullest extent possible. If we are to have a free market in education with the consumer presented with an attractive range of "choice," a national curriculum and especially national testing in essence act as a "state watchdog committee" to control the "worst excesses" of the market.[40]

However, let us be honest to our own history here. Even with the supposed emphasis on portfolios and other more flexible forms of evaluation by some educators, there is no evidence at all to support the hope that what ultimately and permanently will be installed— even if only because of time and expense—will be anything other than a system of mass standardized paper and pencil tests.

Yet, we also must be absolutely clear about the social function of such a proposal. A national curriculum may be seen as a device for accountability, to help us establish benchmarks so that parents can evaluate schools. But it also puts into motion a system in which children themselves will be ranked and ordered as never before. One of its primary roles will be to act as "a mechanism for differentiating children more rigidly against fixed norms, *the social meanings and derivation of which are not available for scrutiny*."[41]

Thus, while the proponents of a national curriculum may see it as a means to create social cohesion and to give all of us the capacity to improve our schools by measuring them against "objective" criteria, the effects will be the opposite. The criteria may seem objective; but the results will not be, given existing differences in resources and in class and race segregation. Rather than leading to cultural and social cohesion, differences between "we" and the "others" will be socially produced even more strongly, and the attendant social antagonisms and cultural and economic destruction will worsen. (This applies also to the current infatuation with outcome-based education, a new term for older versions of educational control and stratification.)

Richard Johnson helps us understand the social processes at work here.

> This nostalgia for "cohesion" is interesting, but the great delusion is that all pupils—black and white, working class, poor, and middle-class, boys and girls—will receive the curriculum in the same way. Actually, it will be read in different ways, according to how pupils are placed in social relationships and culture. A common curriculum, in a heterogeneous society, is not a recipe for "cohesion", but for resistance and the renewal of divisions. Since it always rests on cultural foundations of its own, it will put pupils in their places, not according to "ability", but according to how their cultural communities rank along the criteria taken as the "standard". A curriculum which does not "explain itself", is not ironical or self-critical, will always have this effect. [42]

These are significant points, especially the call for all curricula to *explain themselves*. In complex societies like our own, ones riven with differential power, the only kind of "cohesion" that is possible is one in which we overtly recognize differences and inequalities. The curriculum then should not be presented as "objective." Rather, it must constantly *subjectify* itself. That is, it must "acknowledge its own roots" in the culture, history, and social interests out of which it arose. Accordingly, it will homogenize neither this culture, history, and social interest, nor the students. The "same treatment" by sex, race and ethnicity, or class is not the same at all. A democratic curriculum and pedagogy must begin with a recognition of "the different social positionings and cultural repertoires in the classrooms, and the power relations between them." Thus, if we are concerned with "really equal treatment"—as I think we must be—we must base a curriculum on a recognition of those differences that empower and depower our students in identifiable ways. [43]

Foucault reminded us that if you want to understand how power works, look at the margins, look at the knowledge, self-understandings, and struggles of those whom powerful groups in this society have cast off as "the other." [44] The New Right and its allies have created entire groups as these "others"—people of color, women who refuse to accept external control of their lives and bodies, gays and lesbians, the poor, and, as I know from my own biography, the vibrant culture of working class life (and the list could go on). It is in the recognition of these differences that curriculum dialogue can go on. Such a national dialogue begins with the concrete and public exploration of "how we are differently positioned in society and culture." What the New Right embargoes—the knowledge of the margins, of how culture and power are indissolubly linked—becomes a set of indispensable resources here.[45]

The proposed national curriculum, of course, would recognize some of these differences. But, as Linda Christian-Smith and I argue in *The Politics of the Textbook*, the national curriculum serves both to partly acknowledge difference and at the same time to recuperate it back within the supposed consensus that exists about what we should teach.[46] It is part of an attempt to recreate hegemonic power that has been partly fractured by social movements.

The very idea of a common culture upon which a national curriculum—as defined by neoconservatives—is to be built is itself a form of cultural politics. In the immense linguistic, cultural, and religious diversity that makes up the constant creativity and flux in which we live, it is the cultural policy of the Right to "override" such diversity. Thinking it is reinstituting a common culture, instead it is *inventing* one, in much the same way as E. D. Hirsch has tried to do in his self-parody of what it means to be literate.[47] A uniform culture never truly existed in the United States, only a selective version, an invented tradition that is reinstalled (though in different forms) in times of economic crisis and a crisis in authority relations, both of which threaten the hegemony of the culturally and economically dominant.

The expansion of voices in the curriculum and the vehement responses of the Right become crucial here. Multicultural and antiracist curricula present challenges to the program of the New Right, challenges that go to the core of their vision. A largely monocultural national curriculum (which deals with diversity by centering the always ideological "we" and usually then simply mentioning "the contributions" of people of color, women, and "others," or by creating a false logic of equivalence in which "we are all immigrants") emphasizes the maintenance of existing hierarchies of what counts as official knowledge, the revivifying of traditional "Western" standards and values, the return to a "disciplined" (and one could say largely masculinist) pedagogy, and so on. A threat to any of these is also a threat to the entire world view of the Right.[48]

The idea of a "common culture"—in the guise of the romanticized Western tradition of the neoconservatives (or even as expressed in the longings of some socialists)—does not give enough thought, then, to the immense cultural heterogeneity of a society that draws its cultural traditions from all over the world. The task of defending public education as *public*, as deserving of widespread support "across an extremely diverse and deeply divided people, involves a lot more than restoration."[49]

The debate in England is similar. A national curriculum is seen by the Right as essential to prevent relativism. For most of its proponents, a common curriculum basically must transmit both the "common culture" and the high culture that has grown out of it. Anything else will result in incoherence, no culture, merely a "void." Thus, a national culture is "defined in exclusive, nostalgic, and frequently racist terms."[50] Richard Johnson's analysis of this process documents its social logic.

> In formulations like these, culture is thought of as a homogeneous way of life or tradition, not as a sphere of difference, relationships, or power. No recognition is given to the real diversity of social orientations and cultures within a given nation-state or people. Yet a selective version of a national culture is installed as an absolute condition for any social identity at all. The borrowing, mixing and fusion of elements from different cultural systems, a commonplace everyday practice in societies like [ours], is unthinkable within this framework, or is seen as a kind of cultural misrule that will produce nothing more than a void. So the "choices" are between . . . a national culture or no culture at all.[51]

The racial subtext here is perhaps below the surface, but is still present in significant ways.[52]

There are many more things that could be said. However, one thing is perfectly clear: The national curriculum is a mechanism for the political control of knowledge.[53] In order to fully understand this, we must recognize its underlying logic of false consensus. Once established, there will be little chance of turning back. It may be modified by the conflicts that its content generates, but it is in its very establishment that its politics lies. Once established, it undoubtedly will harden as it becomes linked to a massive system of national testing. When this is connected to the other parts of the rightist agenda—marketization and privatization—there is sufficient reason to give us pause, especially given the increasingly powerful conservative gains at local, regional, and state levels.

## WHO BENEFITS?

One final question remains, one that I hinted at previously. Since leadership in such efforts to "reform" our educational system and its curriculum, teaching, and evaluative policies and practices is largely exercised by the rightist coalition, we need always to ask, "Whose reforms are these?" and "Who benefits?"

This is indeed reform on the cheap. A system of national curricula and national testing cannot help but ratify and exacerbate gender, race, and class differences in the absence of sufficient resources both human and material. Thus, when the fiscal crisis in most of our urban areas is so severe that classes are being held in gymnasiums and hallways, when many schools do not have enough funds to stay open for the full 180 days a year, when buildings are literally disintegrating before our very eyes,[54] when in some cities three classrooms must share one set of textbooks at the elementary level,[55]—and I could go on—it is simply a flight of fantasy to assume that more standardized testing and national curriculum guidelines are the answer. As shall be demonstrated in Chapter 4, with the destruction of the economic infrastructure of these same cities through capital flight, with youth unemployment at nearly 75% in many of them, with almost nonexistent health care, and with lives that are often devoid of hope for meaningful mobility because of what simply might best be called the pornography of poverty, to assume that establishing curricular benchmarks based on problematic cultural visions, along with more rigorous testing, will do more than affix labels to poor students in a way that is seemingly more neutral, is to totally misunderstand the situation. It will lead to more blame being attached to students and poor parents and especially to the schools that they attend. It also will be very expensive to institute. Enter voucher and "choice" plans with even wider public approval.

Basil Bernstein's analysis of the complexities of this situation and of its ultimate results is more than a little useful here. As he says, "The pedagogic practices of the new vocationalism [neoliberalism] and those of the old autonomy of knowledge [neoconservatism] represent a conflict between different elitist ideologies, one based on the class hierarchy of the market and the other based on the hierarchy of knowledge and its class supports."[56] Whatever the oppositions between market- and knowledge-oriented pedagogic and curricular practices, present racial, gender, and class-based inequalities are likely to be reproduced.[57]

What Bernstein calls an "autonomous visible pedagogy"—one that relies on overt standards and highly structured models of teaching and evaluation—justifies itself by referring to its intrinsic worthiness. The value of the acquisition of, say, the "Western tradition" lies in its foundational status for "all we hold dear" and in the norms and dispositions that it instills in students.

> Its arrogance lies in its claim to moral high ground and to the superiority of its culture, its indifference to its own stratification consequences, its conceit in its lack of relation to anything other than itself, its self-referential abstracted autonomy.[58]

Its supposed opposite—based on the knowledge, skills, and dispositions "required" by business and industry and with the aim of transforming schooling around market principles—is actually a much more complex ideological construction.

> It incorporates some of the criticism of the autonomous visible pedagogy . . . criticism of the failure of the urban school, of the passivity and inferior status [given to] parents, of the boredom of . . . pupils and their consequent disruptions of and resistance to irrelevant curricula, of assessment procedures which itemize relative failure rather than the positive strength of the acquirer. But it assimilates these criticisms into a new discourse: a new pedagogic Janus. . . . The explicit commitment to greater choice by parents . . . is not a celebration of participatory democracy, but a thin cover for the old stratification of schools and curricula.[59]

Are Bernstein's conclusions correct? Will the combination of national curricula, testing, and privatization actually lead away from democratic processes and outcomes? Here we must look not to Japan (where many people unfortunately have urged us to look) but to Britain, where this combination of proposals is much more advanced.

In Britain, there is now considerable evidence that the overall effects of the various market-oriented policies introduced by the rightist government are *not* genuine pluralism or the "interrupting [of] traditional modes of social reproduction." On the contrary, they may instead provide largely "a legitimating gloss for the perpetuation of long-standing forms of structured inequality."[60] The fact that one of their major effects has been the depowering and deskilling of large numbers of teachers also is not inconsequential.[61]

Edwards, Gewirtz, and Whitty, who take the argument even further, have come to similar conclusions. In essence, the rightist preoccupation with "escape routes" diverts attention from the effects of such policies on those (probably the majority) who will be left behind.[62]

Thus, it is indeed possible—actually probable—that market-oriented approaches in education (even when coupled with a strong state over a system of national curricula and testing) will exacerbate already existing and widespread class and race divisions. "Freedom" and "choice" in the new educational market will be for those who can afford them. "Diversity" in schooling simply will be a more polite word for the condition of educational apartheid.[63]

### RETHINKING COMMON CULTURE

I have been more than a little negative in my appraisal here. I have argued that the politics of official knowledge—in this case surrounding proposals for a national curriculum and national testing—cannot be fully understood in an isolated way. All of this needs to be situated directly in larger ideological dynamics in which we are seeing an attempt by a new hegemonic bloc to transform our very ideas of what education is for. This transformation involves a major shift—one that Dewey would have shuddered at—in which democracy becomes an economic rather than a political concept, and where the idea of the public good withers at its very roots.

But perhaps I have been too negative. Perhaps there are good reasons to support national curricula and national testing, even as currently constituted, precisely *because* of the power of the rightist coalition.

It is possible, for example, to argue that *only* by establishing a national curriculum and national testing can we stop the fragmentation that will accompany the neoliberal portion of the rightist project. Only such a system would protect the very idea of a *public* school, would protect teachers' unions (which in a privatized and marketized system would lose much of their power), and would protect poor children and children of color from the vicissitudes of the market. After all, it is the "free market" that created the poverty and destruction of community that they are experiencing in the first place.

It is also possible to argue, as Geoff Whitty has in the British case, that the very fact of a national curriculum encourages both the formation of intense public debate about whose knowledge is declared official and the creation of progressive coalitions across a variety of differences against such state-sponsored definitions of legitimate knowledge.[64] It could be the vehicle for the *return* of the political that the Right so wishes to evacuate from our public discourse and that the efficiency experts wish to make into merely a technical concern.

Thus, it is quite possible that the establishment of a national curriculum could have the effect of unifying oppositional and oppressed groups. Given the fragmented nature of progressive educational movements today, and given a system of school financing and governance that forces groups to focus largely on the local or state level, one function of a national curriculum could be the coalescence of groups around a common agenda. A *national* movement for a more democratic vision of school reform could be the result.

In many ways—and I am very serious here—we owe principled conservatives (and there are many) a debt of gratitude in an odd way. It is their realization that curriculum issues are not only about techniques, about how-tos, that has helped stimulate the current debate. When many women, people of color, and labor organizations (these groups obviously are not mutually exclusive) fought for decades to have society recognize the selective tradition in official knowledge, these movements often (though not always) were silenced, ignored, or recuperated into dominant discourses.[65] The power of the Right—in its contradictory attempt to establish a national common culture, to challenge what is now taught, and to make that culture part of a vast supermarket of choices and thus purge cultural politics from our sensibilities—has made it impossible for the politics of official knowledge to be ignored.

Should we then support a national curriculum and national testing to keep total privatization and marketization at bay? Under current conditions, I do not think it is worth the risk—not only because of the extensive destructive potential in the long and short run, but also because I think it misconstrues and reifies the issues of a common curriculum and a common culture.

Here I must repeat the arguments I made in the second edition of *Ideology and Curriculum*.[66] The current call to "return" to a "common culture" in which all students are to be given the values of a specific group—usually the dominant group—does not in my mind concern a common culture at all. Such an approach hardly scratches the surface of the political and educational issues involved. A common culture can never be the general extension to everyone of what a minority mean and believe. Rather, and crucially, it requires not the stipulation of the facts, concepts, skills, and values that make us all "culturally literate," *but the creation of the conditions necessary for all people to participate in the creation and re-creation of meanings and values*. It requires a democratic process in which all people—not simply those who are the intellectual guardians of the "Western tradition"—can be involved in the deliberation over what is important. It should go without saying that this necessitates the removal of the very real material obstacles— unequal power, wealth, time for reflection—that stand in the way of such participation. [67] As Raymond Williams so perceptively put it:

> The idea of a common culture is in no sense the idea of a simply consent- ing, and certainly not of a merely conforming society. [It involves] a common determination of meanings by all the people, acting sometimes as individuals, sometimes as groups, in a process which has no particu- lar end, and which can never be supposed at any time to have finally realized itself, to have become complete. In this common process, the only absolute will be the keeping of the channels and institutions of communication clear so that all may contribute, and be helped to con- tribute. [68]

In speaking of a common culture, then, we should *not* be talking of something uniform, something to which we all conform. Instead, what we should be asking is "precisely, for that free, contributive and common *process* of participation in the creation of meanings and values." [69] It is the very blockage of that process in our institutions that must concern all of us.

Our current language speaks to how this process is being defined during the conservative restoration. Instead of people who partici- pate in the struggle to build and rebuild our educational, cultural, political, and economic relations, we are defined as consumers (of that "particularly acquisitive class type"). This is truly an extraordi- nary concept, for it sees people as either stomachs or furnaces. We use and use up. We don't create. Someone else does that. This is disturbing enough in general, but in education it is truly disabling. Leave it to the guardians of tradition, the efficiency and accountability experts, the holders of "real knowledge," or to the Christopher Whit- tles of this world who will build us franchised "schools of choice" for the generation of profit. [70] Yet, we leave it to these people at great risk to all of us, but especially to those students who are already economically and culturally disenfranchised by our dominant institu- tions.

As I noted at the outset of this chapter, we live in a society with identifiable winners and losers. In the future, we may say that the losers made poor "consumer choices" and, well, that's the way mar- kets operate after all. But is this society really only one vast market?

As Whitty reminds us, in a time when so many people have

found from their daily experiences that the supposed "grand narratives" of progress are deeply flawed, is it appropriate to return to yet another grand narrative, the market?[71] The results of this "narrative" are visible every day in the destruction of our communities and environment, in the increasing racism of society, and in the faces and bodies of our children, who see the future and turn away.

Many people are able to dissociate themselves from these realities. There is almost a pathological distancing among the affluent.[72] Yet, how can one not be morally outraged at the growing gap between rich and poor, the persistence of hunger and homelessness, the deadly absence of medical care, the degradations of poverty? If *this* were the (always self-critical and constantly subjectifying) centerpiece of a national curriculum, perhaps such a curriculum would be worthwhile after all. But then how could it be tested cheaply and efficiently and how could the Right control its ends and means? Until such a time, we can take a rightist slogan made popular in another context and apply it to their educational agenda. What is that slogan? "Just say no."

## CHAPTER 3

# Becoming Right:
# Education and the Formation of
# Conservative Movements

## with Anita Oliver

I ended Chapter 2 with a slightly rhetorical conclusion, urging us to reject the move toward a national curriculum and national testing. Yet perhaps saying no is not totally sufficient. While we may be saying no to the neoliberal emphasis on marketization and privatization and the neoconservative emphasis on strong control over knowledge and values, the rightist alliance is growing measurably stronger. One of the reasons it is gaining such momentum is its ability to integrate under its hegemonic umbrella the sentiments of large numbers of people who believe that schools and many layers of government are "out of touch" and "don't listen." These people are driven by populist understandings, understandings that do contain insights into the nature of power relations in this society. Populist sentiments do not have to become authoritarian. They do not have to become integrated within New Right politics. But in many cases they do. In the process, thousands and thousands of parents who care deeply about their children are convinced to join social movements that will ultimately challenge our accepted forms of curriculum and teaching, and increasingly the very legitimacy of public schools. How this happens is the subject of this chapter.

### UNDERSTANDING RIGHTIST MOVEMENTS

Throughout the United States, national organizations have been formed by conservatives to fight against what counts as "official knowledge" in schools. These organizations often reach out to local groups of "concerned citizens" and offer financial and legal assistance in their battles with school systems at state and local levels. Citizens for Excellence in Education, the Eagle Forum, the Western Center for Law and Religious Freedom, and Focus on the Family are among the most active. Mel and Norma Gabler have developed a system of opposition that aids parents and rightist groups throughout the country in their attempts to challenge educational policies and practices and to either change the content of books or have them removed from schools. The "Christian Right" has become an increasingly powerful movement in the United States, one that has had major effects on educational policy deliberations, curriculum, and teaching.[1]

Yet, it would be all too easy to read these organizations' imprint everywhere. Indeed, this would be a serious mistake not only empirically, but conceptually and politically as well. While there is intentionality, too often we see rightist movements conspiratorially. In the process, we not only reduce the complexity that surrounds the politics of education, but we take refuge in binary oppositions of good and bad. We thereby ignore the elements of possible insight in some (even right-wing) oppositional groups and ignore the places where decisions could have been made that would not have contributed to the growth of these movements.

A basic question undergirding this chapter is this: How does the religious right grow? Our claim is that this can be fully understood only by focusing on the interactions, ones that often occur at a local level, between the state and the daily lives of ordinary people as they interact with institutions.

In no way do we wish to minimize the implications of the growth of rightist social movements. Indeed, the conservative restoration has had truly negative effects on the lives of millions of people in a number of countries,[2] effects that, as was shown in the previous chapter, could prove deeply damaging. Rather, we want to provide a more dynamic view of how and why such movements actually are found to be attractive. Too often, not only do current analyses assume what has to be explained, but they place all of the blame for the growth of rightist positions on the persons who "become Right." No one focuses on the larger sets of relations that might push people toward a more aggressive right-wing stance. Yet, this is exactly our point. People often "become Right" due to their interactions with unresponsive institutions. Thus, part of our argument is that there is a close connection between how the state is structured and acts, and the formation of social movements and identities.

In what follows, we combine elements of neo-Gramscian and poststructural analyses. Our aim is partly to demonstrate how the former—with its focus on the state, on the formation of hegemonic blocs, on new social alliances, and the generation of consent—and the latter—with its focus on the local, on the formation of subjectivity and identity, and on the creation of subject positions—can creatively work together to illuminate crucial parts of the politics of education.[3] Behind this analysis is a particular position on what critical research should do.

In other publications, one of us has argued that in all too much of the current critically and oppositionally oriented literature in education, "our words have taken on wings." That is, theoretical layer upon theoretical layer is added without coming to grips with the real and existing complexities of schooling. This is *not* an argument against theory. Rather, it takes the position that our eloquent abstractions are weakened in the extreme if they do not get formed in relationship to the supposed object of these abstractions—schooling and its economic, political, and cultural conditions of existence. Letting the daily life surrounding the politics of educational institutions rub against you is wholly salutary in this regard. In the absence of this, all too many "critical educational theorists" coin trendy neologisms but remain all too disconnected from the lives and struggles of real people in real institutions.[4] We hope to overcome that here.


"ACCIDENTAL" FORMATIONS

As Whitty, Edwards, and Gewirtz document in their analysis of the growth of conservative initiatives such as city technology colleges in England, rightist policies and their effects are not always the result of carefully planned initiatives.[5] They often have an accidental quality to them. This is not to deny intentionality. Rather, the historical specificities of local situations and the complexities of multiple power relations in each site mean that conservative policies are highly mediated and have unforeseen consequences. If this is the case for many instances of overt attempts at moving educational policy and practice in a conservative direction, it is even more true when we examine how rightist sentiments grow among local actors. Most analyses of "the Right" assume a number of things. They all too often assume a unitary ideological movement, seeing it as a relatively uncontradictory group rather than a complex assemblage of different tendencies many of which are in a tense and unstable relationship to each other. Many analyses also take "the Right" as a "fact," as a given. It already exists as a massive structuring force that is able to work its way into daily life and into our discourses in well-planned ways. This takes for granted one of the most important questions that needs to be investigated: How does the Right get *formed*?

In Chapter 2, it was argued that rightist policies are often compromises both between the Right and other groups and among the various tendencies within the conservative alliance. Thus, neoliberals, neoconservatives, authoritarian populist fundamentalist religious groups, and a particular fraction of the new middle class all have found a place under the ideological umbrella provided by broad rightist tendencies. It also was shown how conservative discourses act in creative ways to disarticulate prior connections and rearticulate groups of people into this larger ideological movement by connecting to the real hopes, fears, and conditions of people's daily lives and by providing seemingly "sensible" explanations for the current troubles people are having.[6] Yet, this too gives the impression that the creative educational project that the Right is engaged in—to convince considerable numbers of people to join the broader alliance—works its way to the local level in smooth, rational steps. This may not be the case.

We want to argue that much more mundane experiences and events often underlie the rightist turn at a local level. While the Right *has* engaged in concerted efforts to move our discourse and practices in particular directions, its success in convincing people is dependent on those things that Whitty, Edwards, and Gewirtz have called "accidents." Of course, "accidents" are often patterned and are themselves the results of complex relations of power. But the point is still a telling one. Acceptance of conservative tendencies is *built*—not always in planned ways—and may involve tensions and contradictory sentiments among the people who ultimately "become Right."

In illuminating this, first we shall describe more deeply the assemblage of cultural assumptions, fears, and tensions that underpin the cultural and religious right in the United States.[7] We then shall argue that the ways in which the bureaucratic state has developed are ideally suited to confirm these fears and tensions. Third, we shall instantiate these arguments by focusing on a specific case in which a textbook controversy led to the formation of rightist sentiments in a local community. Finally, we want to suggest a number of important implications of this analysis for the politics of education and for attempts at countering the growth of ultra-rightist movements in education.


## A WORLD OF DANGER

There is a story told by a teacher about a discussion that arose in her elementary school classroom. A number of students were excitedly talking about some "dirty words" that had been scribbled on the side of a building during Halloween. Even after the teacher asked the children to get ready for their language arts lesson, most of them continued to talk about "those words." As often happens, the teacher sensed that this could not be totally ignored. She asked her students what *made* words "dirty." This provoked a long and productive discussion among these second graders about how certain words were used to hurt people and how "this wasn't very nice."

Throughout it all, one child had not said a thing, but was clearly deeply involved in listening. Finally, he raised his hand and said that he knew "the dirtiest word in the world." He was too embarrassed to say the word out loud (and also knew that it would be inappropriate to even utter it in school). The teacher asked him to come up later and whisper it in her ear. During recess, he came over to the teacher, put his head close to hers and quietly, secretly, said "the word." The teacher almost broke up with laughter. The dirty word, that word that could never be uttered, was "statistics." One of the boy's parents worked for a local radio station and every time the ratings came out, the parent would angrily state, "Those damn statistics!" What could be dirtier?

For large numbers of parents and conservative activists, other things are a lot "dirtier." Discussions of the body, of sexuality, of politics and personal values, and of any of the social issues surrounding these topics, are a danger zone. To deal with them in any way in school is not wise. But if they are going to be dealt with, these conservative activists demand that they must be handled in the context of traditional gender relations, the nuclear family, and the "free-market" economy, and according to sacred texts like the Bible.

Take sexuality education as a case in point. For cultural conservatives, sex education is one of the ultimate forms of "secular humanism" in schools. It is attacked by the New Right both as a major threat to parental control of schools and because of its teaching of "nontraditional" values. For the coalition of forces that make up the New Right, sex education can destroy the family and religious morality "by encouraging masturbation, premarital sex, lots of sex, sex without guilt, sex for fun, homosexual sex, sex."[8] These groups view it as education for, not about, sex, which will create an obsession that can override "Christian morality" and threaten God-given gender roles.[9] These were important elements in the intense controversy over the Rainbow Curriculum in New York City, for example, and certainly contributed to the successful moves to oust the city's school superintendent from his position.

The vision of gender roles that stands behind these attacks is striking. Allen Hunter, one of the most perceptive commentators on the conservative agenda, argues that the New Right sees the family as an organic and divine unity that "resolves male egoism and female selflessness."[10] As he goes on to say:

> Since gender is divine and natural . . . there is [no] room for legitimate political conflict. . . . Within the family women and men—stability and dynamism—are harmoniously fused when undisturbed by modernism, liberalism, feminism, [and] humanism which not only threaten masculinity and femininity directly, but also [do so] through their effects on children and youth. . . . "Real women," i.e. women who know themselves to be wives *and* mothers, will not threaten the sanctity of the home by striving for self. When men or women challenge these gender roles they break with God and nature; when liberals, feminists, and secular humanists prevent them from fulfilling these roles they undermine the divine and natural supports upon which society rests.[11]

All of this is connected to their view that public schooling *itself* is a site of immense danger.[12] In the words of conservative activist Tim La Haye, "Modern public education is the most dangerous force in a child's life: religiously, sexually, economically, patriotically, and physically."[13] This is connected to the cultural conservative's sense of loss surrounding schooling and community.

> Until recently, as the New Right sees it, schools were extensions of home and traditional morality. Parents could entrust their children to public schools because they were locally controlled and reflected Biblical and parental values. However, taken over by alien, elitist forces schools now interpose themselves between parents and children. Many people experience fragmentation of the unity between family, church, and school as a loss of control of daily life, one's children, and America. Indeed, [the New Right] argues that parental control of education is Biblical, for "in God's plan, the primary responsibility for educating the young lies in the home and directly in the father."[14]

Here it is clearly possible to see why, say, sexuality education has become such a major issue for conservative movements. Its very existence, and especially its most progressive and honest moments, threatens crucial elements of the entire world view of these parents and activists.

Of course, issues of sexuality, gender, and the body are not the only focus of attention of cultural conservatives. These concerns are linked to a much larger array of questions about what counts as "legitimate" content in schools. And in this larger arena of concern about the entire corpus of school knowledge, conservative activists have had no small measure of success in pressuring textbook publishers and in altering aspects of state educational policy as well. This is critical, since the text still remains the dominant definition of the curriculum in schools not only in the United States but in many other nations as well.[15]

The power of these groups can be seen in the "self-censorship" in which publishers engage. For instance, a number of publishers of high school literature anthologies have chosen to include Martin Luther King's "I Have a Dream" speech, but *only* after all references to the intense racism of the United States have been removed.[16]

Another example is provided by the textbook law in Texas, which mandates texts that stress patriotism, authority, and the discouragement of "deviance." Since most textbook publishers aim the content and organization of their texts at what will be approved in a small number of populous states that in essence approve and purchase their texts *statewide*, this gives Texas (and California) immense power in determining what will count as legitimate knowledge throughout the entire country.[17]

Quoting from the Texas legislation on textbooks, the author of a recent study of textbook controversy describes it in this way:

> "Textbook content shall promote citizenship and understanding of the essentials and benefits of the free enterprise system, emphasizing patriotism and respect for recognized authority, and promote respect for individual rights." Textbooks shall not "include selections or works which encourage or condone civil disobedience, social strife, or disregard of law," nor shall they "contain material which serves to undermine authority" or "which would cause embarrassing situations or interference in the learning atmosphere of the classroom." Finally, textbooks approved for use in Texas "shall not encourage lifestyles deviating from generally accepted standards of society." The Texas law's endorsement of free enterprise and traditional lifestyles and its prohibition of lawlessness and rebellion are regularly cited by textbook activists

to support their efforts to remove material which, in their view, promotes socialism, immorality or disobedience. [18]

Clearly here, with the Texas law's emphasis on "traditional lifestyles," we can see that the "family" stands as the building block of society, "the foundation upon which all of culture is maintained." It provides civilization with its moral foundation. The family's strength and stability, in essence, determine the vitality and moral life of the larger society. [19] One of the ways it guarantees this is through its central place in instilling children with the proper moral values and traits of character that can withstand the "moral decay" seen all around us.

Yet, it is not only the family's place as a source of moral authority that is important here. The family, and the "traditional" gender roles within it, demands that "people act for the larger good" by taming the pursuit of self-interest that is so powerful in the (supposedly) male public world. [20] Rebecca Klatch notes that

> Implicit in this image of the family is the social conservative conception of human nature. Humans are creatures of unlimited appetites and instincts. Left on their own, they would turn the world into a chaos of seething passions, overrun by narrow self-interest. Only the moral authority of the family or the church restrains human passions, transforming self-interest into the larger good. The ideal society is one in which individuals are integrated into a moral community, bound together by faith, by common moral values, and by obeying the dictates of the family, church, and God. [21]

In this way of constructing the world, *all* of the nation's problems are attributed to moral decay. The signs of decay are everywhere: "sexual promiscuity, pornography, legalized abortion, and the displacement of marriage, family, and motherhood." [22] Even widespread poverty is at base a moral problem, but not in the way progressives might see this: as the results of social policies that have little ethical concern for their effects on the poor and working class. Rather, as George Gilder put it in a speech at the conservative activist Phyllis Schlafly's celebration of the ultimate defeat of the Equal Rights Amendment, "The crucial problems of the poor in America are *not* material. This is something [we] must understand. The poor in America are richer than the upper fifth of all people during most of America's history. They are some of the richest people in the world. The crucial problems of the poor are not material but spiritual." [23] Given this definition of the problem, poverty and other aspects of moral decay so visible in our major institutions such as schools can be solved only through moral renewal, prayer, repentance, and a clear recognition of the centrality of religious belief, morality, and "decency."[24]

We should not take lightly the view of schooling that such movements espouse—or the perception of reality that lies behind this view. Perhaps this perception can best be seen in a letter circulated to conservative parents and activists by the Eagle Forum, one of the most active rightist groups associated with Phyllis Schlafly. Similar letters have been circulated throughout school systems in the United States. It takes the form of a formal notification to school boards about parents' rights.

> To:   School Board President
> Dear _____
>     I am the parent of _____ who attends _____ School. Under U.S. legislation and court decisions, parents have the primary responsibility for their children's education, and pupils have certain rights which the schools may not deny. Parents have the right to assure that their children's beliefs and moral values are not undermined by the schools. Pupils have the right to have and to hold their values and moral standards without direct or indirect manipulation by the schools through curricula, textbooks, audio-visual materials, or supplementary assignments.
>     Accordingly, I hereby request that my child be involved in NO school activities or materials listed below unless I have first reviewed all the relevant materials and have given my written consent for their use:
>
> * Psychological and psychiatric examinations, tests, or surveys that are designed to elicit information about attitudes, habits, traits, opinions, beliefs, or feelings of an individual or group.
> * Psychological and psychiatric treatment that is designed to affect behavioral, emotional, or attitudinal characteristics of an individual or group.
> * Values clarification, use of moral dilemmas, discussion of religious or moral standards, role-playing or open-ended discussions of situations involving moral issues, and survival games including life/death decisions exercises.
> * Death education, including abortion, euthanasia, suicide, use of violence, and discussions of death and dying.
> * Curricula pertaining to alcohol and drugs.

- Instruction in nuclear war, nuclear policy, and nuclear classroom games.
- Anti-nationalistic, one-world government or globalism curricula.
- Discussion and testing on interpersonal relationships; discussions of attitudes toward parents and parenting.
- Education in human sexuality, including premarital sex, extramarital sex, contraception, abortion, homosexuality, group sex and marriages, prostitution, incest, masturbation, bestiality, divorce, population control, and roles of males and females; sex behavior and attitudes of student and family.
- Pornography and any materials containing profanity and/or sexual explicitness.
- Guided fantasy techniques; hypnotic techniques; imagery and suggestology.
- Organic evolution, including the idea that man has developed from previous or lower types of living things.
- Discussions of witchcraft and the occult, the supernatural, and Eastern mysticism.
- Political affiliations and beliefs of student and family; personal religious beliefs and practices.
- Mental and psychological problems and self-incriminating behavior potentially embarrassing to the student or family.
- Critical appraisals of other individuals with whom the child has family relationships.
- Legally recognized privileged and analogous relationships, such as those of lawyers, physicians and ministers.
- Income, including the student's role in family activities and finances.
- Non-academic personality tests; questionnaires on personal and family life and attitudes.
- Autobiography assignments; log books, diaries, and personal journals.
- Contrived incidents for self-revelation; sensitivity training, group encounter sessions, talk-ins, magic circle techniques, self-evaluation and auto-criticism; strategies designed for self-disclosure (e.g., zig-zag).
- Sociograms; sociodrama; psychodrama; blindfold walks; isolation techniques.

The purpose of this letter is to preserve my child's rights under the Protection of Pupil Rights Amendment (the Hatch Amendment) to the General Education Provisions Act, and under its regulations as published in the *Federal Register* of Sept. 6, 1984, which became effective Nov. 12, 1984. These regulations provide a procedure for filing complaints first at the local level, and then with the U.S. Department of Education. If a voluntary remedy fails, federal funds can be withdrawn from those in violation of the law. I respectfully ask you to send me a substantive response to this letter attaching a copy of your policy statement on procedures for parental permission requirements, to notify all my child's teachers, and to keep a copy of this letter in my child's permanent file. Thank you for your cooperation.

Sincerely,

It is clear from this letter how much the state is distrusted. Here, schooling *is* a site of immense danger. The range of prohibitions covered documents the sense of alarm these parents and activists feel and why they would closely examine what their children are supposedly experiencing in schools. In the minds of conservatives, raising these objections is not censorship; it is protecting the entire range of things that are at the center of their being.

## STATE FORMATION AND BUREAUCRATIC CONTROL

It is in the conflict over this range of issues that new parts of the state are formed. We often have employed a reified vision of the state. The state is seen as a thing. It is simply there. Yet at all levels, the state is *in formation*. Not only is "it" an arena in which different groups struggle to legitimate and institute their own senses of needs and needs discourses,[25] but it also is itself formed and changed in both its content and form by these struggles.

Throughout the United States at local levels, school districts have established mechanisms to regulate conflict over official knowledge. As we showed, rightist populist social movements, especially Christian fundamentalists, have raised fundamental (no pun intended) objections to an extensive array of curricula, pedagogy, and evaluative procedures. Thus, for example, textbooks in reading and literature have been challenged for their "secular humanism," their sponsorship of "socialism," occultism, their "overemphasis" on minority culture, and even their supposedly veiled espousal of vegetarianism.[26]

Focusing on textbook controversies is crucial in a number of ways. First, in the current absence of an overt and official national curriculum in the United States (although, as we saw, this might be changing), the standardized textbook that is partly regulated by and aimed at widespread state adoption provides much of the framework for a hidden national curriculum.[27] Second, even though many teachers use the textbook as a jumping off point rather than something one must always follow slavishly, teachers in the United States do in fact use the text as the fundamental curriculum artifact in classrooms to a remarkable degree. Third, the absence of a codified national curriculum and the history of populist sentiment here means that many of the most powerful protests over what counts as official knowledge in schools historically have focused on the textbook itself. It provides an ideal fulcrum to pry loose the lid from the dynamics underlying the cultural politics of education and the social movements that form it and are formed by it.

Given the power of these groups, many school districts have offices and/or standardized procedures for dealing "efficiently and safely" with these repeated challenges. One of the effects of such procedures often has been that the institutions construct nearly all challenges to official knowledge in particular ways—as censorship and as coming from organized New Right groups. Thus, the educational apparatus of the state expands as a defensive mechanism to protect itself against such populist pressure. Yet, once this structure is established, its "gaze" defines social criticism in ways it can both understand and deal with. This has crucial theoretical and political implications for how we see the role of the state in the politics of education. For it is in the growth of such bureaucratic procedures and the associated length of time that it takes to rule on challenges that the Right often finds fertile soil. In order to understand this, we need to say more about how we should see the state.

"The state may best be studied as a *process* of rule."[28] In Bruce Curtis's words, state formation involves "the centralization and concentration of relations of economic and political power and authority in society." State formation typically involves the appearance or the reorganization of monopolies over the means of violence, taxation, administration, and *over symbolic systems*.[29] In essence, state formation is about the creation, stabilization, and normalization of relations of power and authority.[30]

Education is not immune to this process. This is part of a much longer history in which the state, through its bureaucratic administration, seeks to keep the "interests of education" not only from the control of elites but also from the influence of populist impulses from below.[31] This is crucial to the story we are telling here.

Bureaucratic systems have substance. Emile Durkheim recognized a century ago that efficiency "is an ethical construct, one whose adoption involves a moral and political choice." The institutionalization of efficiency as a dominant bureaucratic norm is not a neutral technical matter. It is, profoundly, an instance of cultural power relations.[32]

No bureaucracy can function well unless those who interact with it "adopt specific attitudes, habits, beliefs, and orientations." "Proper" attitudes toward authority, "appropriate" beliefs about the legitimacy of expertise, willingness to follow all of the "necessary" rules and procedures—these are crucial to the maintenance of power,[33] even when such power is recognized as acceptable.

This process of freeing the interests of education from elite and popular control was and *is* a crucial element in state formation.[34] The state grows to protect itself and the self-proclaimed "democratic" interests it represents in response to such attempts at control. In the instance of Christian fundamentalists, insurgent cultural forces from below—the "censors"—have created a situation in which the state expands its policing function over knowledge and establishes new bureaucratic offices and procedures to channel dissent into "legitimate" channels.

Curtis puts it exactly correctly when he states that the "standardization and neutralization of judgements [have] tended to make implicit, rather than explicit, the class-specific content of educational governance."[35] Bureaucratic procedures that have been established to promote "the public interest"—and which in some interpretations may do so—are there to try to forge a consensus around and an acceptance of cultural legitimacy that may be rooted in strikingly antagonistic perceptions of the world.

Yet, what happens when these "appropriate" and "proper" beliefs and responses fracture? What happens when the state loses its hold on legitimate authority, when its clients—in interaction with it over a period of time—come to refuse its monopoly over what counts as legitimate symbolic authority?

To answer these questions, we turn to how this dynamic works out in the real world by focusing on the conflict over a textbook series in a local school district where the parties in contention became immensely polarized and where populist pressure from below increasingly turned actively conservative. In the process, we shall show

how the workings of the bureaucratic state paradoxically provide fertile ground for parents to "become Right."

### PROFESSIONALS AND CENSORS

The site of this study, which we shall call Citrus Valley, is a semirural community of about 30,000 people now within commuting distance of several larger western cities because of the growth of the Interstate highway system.[36] It is in the midst of a building boom that is predicted to almost double the population of the area. This is likely to change the atmosphere from that of a quiet, slow-moving, rural community to one resembling a small, faster-paced city. Much of its growing population will likely consist of commuters.

The average household income in 1989, at the beginning of the controversy, was estimated to be $23,500. Demographic data indicate that nearly one-fourth of the current population are between the ages of 65 and 79. The many "senior citizens," and the approximately 50 trailer parks, suggest that Citrus Valley is seen by many people as an attractive place to retire as well.

There are no large industries in Citrus Valley, but the city would certainly like some to move in. In fact, the largest single employer is the school district, with just under 600 employees half of whom are teachers. In 1980, 72% of the adult residents over age 25 had a high school education or less. Approximately 10% had graduated from college. A significant portion of the residents with college degrees work for the school district. The population of Citrus Valley is 95% European American, with a slowly growing Latino population. It is primarily a working class community, but one with a clearly growing and increasingly visible commuter middle class.

Even with the growth of commuting, a large portion of the townspeople are lifetime residents. One person described the community as follows: "People, it's a real ethic here. People believe in traditional values. And they believe in responsibility and working as a community."

Certain things are evident in this brief demographic description. One is the changing nature of class relations in the community. People are moving out of the large metropolitan area newly within commuting distance of Citrus Valley. Fears of violence, a search for "better schools," lower housing prices, and other elements are producing a situation in which members of the new middle class are becoming increasingly visible in the town. This class fraction is noted for its sympathy for child-centered pedagogy and for what Basil Bernstein has called loosely framed and loosely classified curriculum and teaching.[37] Thus, a tension between "country" and "city" and between class-related educational visions may lie beneath the surface.

Second, the changing nature of the community is occurring at a time of perceived fears of downward mobility and a very real economic crisis in the United States where many western states—and the one in which Citrus Valley is located in particular—are experiencing economic dislocation and its attendant apprehensions about the future. Needless to say, farm economies certainly are not immune to these fears and dislocations. For many individuals, this will have a profound impact on their sense of what schooling is for, on what should and should not be taught, and on who should control it. For many working class women and men, economic anxieties and fears of cultural collapse are rightly difficult to separate.

In the middle of these transformations and the possible tensions that underlie the town's outward tranquility and "tradition," the school district has decided to move to a new orientation in its language arts program. In this, it was following the guidelines and timetable laid out by the state's Department of Education for all school districts. The state guidelines strongly urged school districts to use a literature-based approach to teaching language arts, and in fact Citrus Valley had already begun employing such an approach, based on a core of books chosen by the teachers themselves. Both teachers and administrators were enthusiastic about what they perceived as the initial success of their literature/whole language emphasis. The logical step for them was to search for a textbook series that would complement the goals and practices already partly in place.

This particular state allocates funds for purchases of state-adopted material—largely textbooks that have passed through the complicated political and educational screening process necessary for winning approval as a recommended text by the State Board. Seventy percent of the allocations must be spent on such recommended texts, while the majority of the remaining money may be used to purchase nonadopted supplementary material. School districts may use their own funds as well to buy nonadopted material, but in a time of fiscal crisis this is considerably more difficult. Thus, money is available largely for commercially produced and standardized textbooks. The task is to find ones that come closest to the approach one believes in.

Yet, there are many such texts available. To make it more likely that a particular textbook will be chosen, inducements often are offered by publishers. The amount of "free" materials, for instance, given to school districts by a publisher is often considerable. This is common practice among publishers, since textbook publishing is a highly competitive enterprise.[38] In the case of Citrus Valley, the ''gift'' of such free material seemed to have an impact on the choice.

Citrus Valley began the process of selecting a new language arts textbook series in the 1988–89 school year. This was the year for changing reading/language arts textbooks as school districts sought to accommodate revised state guidelines for introducing new series. The result of this process was the selection of the *Impressions* reading series, published by Holt, Rinehart and Winston. The series uses a whole language, literature-based methodology—one grounded in a loosely classified curriculum orientation—which this particular state strives to implement in all schools.

When school began in the fall of 1989, there was no reason to suspect that there would be any problems with *Impressions*, although it *had* been challenged in other districts in this state and in other states as well. After all, the steps for piloting and implementing a new series had been followed carefully. The district introduced the new series with confidence and enthusiasm. The memos circulated around the district after the selection of *Impressions* reflected the pleasure, after much effort, of finally having made a choice that seemed in tune with the district's goals. In June, after telling the teachers that close to 150 boxes of the new books had arrived, one district administrator made a prophetic statement. She wrote, ''Have a wonderful summer! We have an exciting next year in store for us.'' Truer words have never been spoken.

Within the first 2 months of the school year, some parents and teachers began to complain about the books. Parents became concerned about the content of the texts. Not only were the stories ''scary,'' but there were concerns about some of the values in them and also about mistakes in spelling and printing. The parents objected to a number of the selections. For example, one poem from a fifth-grade book was about pigs in a swamp near some houses. The pigs ''live on dead fish and rotting things, drowned pets, plastic and assorted excreta.'' The poem ends with the pigs having consumed the flesh in the pond, and having acquired a taste for flesh they look toward the shore. The district explained that the poem carried an environmental message. For the parents, it was violent and fearful, a claim they made even more strongly about some of the other material in the books for even younger children.

Parents began talking to each other and slowly a more organized sense began to emerge as community members went to school board meetings and had meetings in local churches. Ultimately, a group of parents formed Concerned Citizens of Citrus Valley (cccv) in an effort to convince the school board to withdraw the series. The board and the school administration acted in two paradoxical ways. They treated the challenge as nearly an act of aggression. In essence, they "geared up for war." At the same time, they slowed the process of challenge down by channeling it through the bureaucratic procedures that had been developed—for very good reasons—in many districts, so that teachers and administrators could be protected from outside attacks. In this way, "proper attitudes" and efficient procedures are wedded in the local state's response.

Nearly every parent who was interviewed and who also opposed the books stated that their original introduction to the content of the textbooks began when their child came home and was made upset by a particular selection in the texts. As they organized, cccv parents were unwilling to be identified with outside groups. They felt that their intelligence was being questioned when supporters of the books accused the cccv of being controlled by "outside forces." According to them, when their children brought home disturbing stories that, say, caused nightmares or frightened them, the parents' first reaction was disbelief. Textbooks were "innocuous." Thus, they were more than a little surprised to read stories in their children's books that seemed inappropriate, and were even more surprised and dismayed by what they felt was the board's and the administration's "heavy handed" response.[39]

As the conflict grew, cccv organized a recall campaign against a number of board members. The school system dug in its heels against "far right censors" and the community itself was badly split. For the board and the school administration, the cccv was a symptom of a larger national censorious movement organized around a far right agenda. "Giving in" meant surrendering one's professional expertise to the forces of political reaction. For the cccv, the issue increasingly became one of parental power and of an arrogant school board and school bureaucracy that refused to take citizens' complaints seriously.

Crucial to understanding the situation here is the fact that the leadership of the cccv began to seek to form connections with the religious right only *after* confronting the district administration and the school board for a long period of time. In fact, the connections were never very strong between the cccv and any outside group. Late in the controversy, one person ultimately did become a liaison between rightist groups, and that person is now firmly cemented within a national organization for "religious rights" and assists in rightist political campaigns. Yet, even here, prior to this controversy this individual was not only uninterested in such causes but was opposed to them.

When the CCCV parents were repeatedly rejected by the local school leadership, they were drawn into the rhetoric and views of the New Right. They felt, rightly or wrongly, that their concerns were minimized and trivialized by both the district administration and the school board from the beginning. Only after they were largely dismissed by the holders of educational authority did they begin looking outside the community for groups who held views similar to their own about the nature of the textbooks that had been implemented in the schools. Organizationally, the CCCV parents remained on their own, but the New Right was increasingly perceived as an ideological ally.

Thus, even when the district made limited attempts, as it did, to convince the protestors of the educational benefits of the new pedagogy and curricula, these efforts were dismissed. One is not likely to subscribe to the views of authorities who are disparaging. The schools' immediate response, then—to treat these parents as far right ideologues who were simply interested in censoring books and teachers—helped create the conditions for the growth of the very ideological movements of which they were so frightened.

## THE CONSTRUCTION OF AN ACTIVE RIGHT

Let us examine this a bit more closely. Most members of the CCCV were what might be called "traditionalists." They, indeed, were wary of change. They did like their community as it was (or at least as they perceived it was). They were opposed to the textbook series because of what they felt was its violence, its capacity to frighten children, and its negativity. By and large, the majority of the community seemed to lean in such a traditional direction. Yet, the CCCV parents saw themselves as trying to find a middle ground between the Right and what they considered the "liberal left." Most of them were quite surprised to find themselves identified as part of the Right. Rather, their self-perception was as "hard working citizens" who wanted to maintain positions that allowed them to conduct their lives as they had been doing in the past. Time and again, they restated the position that they were just "ordinary people" who wanted the best for their children.

The parents who originally organized to oppose the textbooks were people from a variety of religious and political persuasions. There were Catholic, Jewish, "mainstream" Protestant, evangelical and fundamentalist Protestant, Mormon, and nonchurch and agnostic members. Also interesting is the fact that only a few church leaders became involved in the controversy in open support of the CCCV parents. There was little evidence that this was a "fundamentalist" religious issue initially organized either from the outside or by evangelical leaders eager to take on the schools as bastions of secular humanism. In fact, because of the religious diversity and a reluctance to be identified as New Right, many CCCV parents were quite hesitant to hold meetings in a church. However, given the paucity of buildings that were large enough to hold the well-attended public meetings, when a local pastor volunteered his church for CCCV use, it was chosen with caution as the meeting place despite these misgivings.

There were other characteristics, however, that seemed to differentiate CCCV members from others in the community. While they were diverse religiously, in general they did not hold public office and they did not feel that they were part of a network that was central to the community's power relations and daily lives. Many expressed feelings that they were on the fringes of local power. Nor were they economically homogeneous; the group included some local businesspeople and professional as well as working class members.

At the first meeting of the CCCV about 25 to 30 people came. At the second meeting there were 75. As the conflict intensified, 700 people packed into the local church that had been volunteered. Police were stationed at a jammed school board meeting called to discuss the textbooks. The tension was visceral.

In many ways, then, most CCCV parents were in the beginning what might best be called "ordinary middle-of-the-road conservatives" without significant affiliations to rightist activist groups; most did not have a larger ideological or religious agenda that they wished to foist on others. Certainly, they did not see themselves as censorious ideologues who wished to transform the United States into a "Christian nation" and who mistrusted anything that was public.

To reduce the conflict to one of relatively ignorant parents or simple-minded religious fundamentalists trying to use censorship to further the aims of a larger rightist movement is both to misconstrue the ways ordinary actors organize around local struggles and to underestimate these people themselves. Such a position sees "dupes"—puppets—in instances such as this and radically simplifies the complexities of such situations. In many ways, such simplifying views reproduce in our own analyses the stereotypes that were embodied in the responses of the school administration and school board to the issues raised by the parents.

The rapidity with which the district responded in such enormous proportions, as if it were in essence preparing for war, seemed to be the catalyst that actually drove the parents in the direction of rightist groups and caused cccv parents to form a stronger oppositional position than they otherwise might have taken. As soon as the cccv parents challenged the district, the district immediately reduced the issue to one of "censorship." This very construction reduced the complexities to a form that was both familiar to the "professional" discourse of school administrators and teachers and enabled the district to respond in ways that did not leave open other interpretations of the motivations and concerns of the parents.

At the beginning of this controversy, information was shared by women talking to women in public places and in their homes. Mothers told each other about the contents of the books when they picked up their children after school, as they met for lunch, and while they visited friends. (As the controversy developed, however, more men became involved and exerted more leadership, highlighting the consistent relationship between gender and the public sphere.)[40] For some of the women who worked very hard in the cccv group, it was the discounting of their concerns that led even more to their persistence: in getting answers to questions about the textbooks and about the process involved in their selection, and in organizing activities against the books themselves. Their response to the school's resistance and to the local state's definition of them as partly irresponsible was to become even more determined in their efforts to disseminate information about the books. Even though they were not visibly angry and confrontational, and even though they became increasingly strong in their opposition to the series, they were *pushed* into resistance by not being taken seriously.

The women involved in cccv had initial political intuitions, but these were not fully formed in any oppositional sense. They included both social/cultural conservatives and laissez faire conservatives, with the former grounded in a belief in the importance of religiosity, "the family," and "tradition," and the latter grounded in ideas about "individual freedom," "American patriotism," and the "free market," thereby documenting the diversity within even the more moderate conservative positions held. Yet, the most common themes of the cccv women were the sovereignty of the family and the perceived attack on their rights as parents to control their children's education.

Added to this was their perception that *Impressions* did not represent America accurately or sufficiently. However, these women did not begin the controversy in previously defined conscious positions of conservatism. Rather, they were startled at the beginning that there was a problem with the textbooks in their community. Through the months of the conflict, their stances became *formed* and became more clear as a result of having to find a way of making sense out of the schools' response.

Thus, as the conflict deepened, one of the leaders of the cccv became increasingly influenced by Francis Schaeffer, a conservative theologian who supported the idea of absolute truth. As this parent searched for ways of understanding her growing distress, she found Schaeffer's ideas more and more attractive. For Schaeffer, there are "true truths." There are rights and wrongs, basic immutable values, that enable us to know with certainty that some things are absolutely right and other things are absolutely wrong. Without this, according to Schaeffer, there is no Christianity. [41]

Let us take another example of a person deeply involved in cccv, a mother of a child in one of the schools using the textbook series. At the outset, she was not a deeply religious person. She rarely attended church, had no strong loyalties to any one organization, and would have rejected the label of "New Right." Her advice to others involved with her at the beginning was to work with the district and not organize. As her views were directly confronted and challenged by the district and her position stereotyped, she began to look more closely at what she felt she had to do with her opposition to the books. Her views were repeatedly minimized and she was accused of being "right wing." As a result of this, not only did she become a part of the development of the cccv by parents, but at the end of the controversy she became deeply involved with Christian women's groups on national political issues. What began as a concern over the content of books, ended with individuals like her becoming active members of right-wing national movements.

At the end of the conflict, the school district announced a "solution." It would continue to use *Impressions* and its core literature program. It would also allow (continue, actually) the practice of allowing parents to request up to two alternative assignments to these materials each semester. It then went further. The district implemented alternative classes for the children of those parents who had become totally opposed to *Impressions*. Parents were asked to reply to a letter in which they were asked if they wanted their children to be in a special non-*Impressions* class. They were told that "this may result in a classroom or school site change for your child. In the event a site change is necessary, you will need to provide transportation."

While this response does show some flexibility on the part of the school system, it immediately created a difficult situation for parents who worked outside the home or who were unable to provide transportation for their children. Work schedules, a lack of two (or even one) cars, economic problems, and other elements created a situation in which parents often had no alternative but to keep their children in the *Impressions* classrooms. Thus were the seeds of further alienation sowed.

As the next school year began, the district reported that 82% of the parents had chosen to put their children in *Impressions* classes. Whether this is evidence of choice or a lack of real alternatives is unclear. Yet, when nearly 20% of parents actively *choose* very different experiences than officially defined knowledge for their children, it is clear that the controversy continues to simmer not too far below the surface.

Other changes were made in the processes by which official knowledge is chosen. For example, parents are now included in the early stages of textbook selection. The school district administrators and the school board are much more aware of the complex politics surrounding parental concerns and the consequences of the "professional" decisions they make. Above all, however, there is a tense watchfulness on all sides and a polarization that deeply divides the community. An active Right now exists in powerful ways.

## IDENTITY POLITICS AND THE STATE

We have been interested here not only in illuminating the complex process through which people become Right, although such analyses are crucial in understanding cultural politics in education, but also in a theoretical agenda. Too often, traditions talk past each other in critical educational studies. Neo-Gramscian, postmodern, and poststructural theories are seen as opposites. We reject these divisions for a more integrative approach. We have taken tools from the neo-Gramscian tradition—an emphasis both on the power of the state and on the ideological currents within common sense, and on the power of cultural movements from below—without ignoring the economic context of social action. We have complemented this with a focus on identity politics and the state's role in circulating subject positions that are then reappropriated by real people in the complex politics of the local level. Behind our approach is a claim that the study of social movements and the conditions of their formation, in a time of increasingly aggressive attacks on the school and on the very idea of "the public" by rightist groups, is essential. Integrating these various perspectives is an ambitious agenda. But the politics of education needs to be treated with the integrative seriousness its complexity deserves.

The implications of what we have described here are of great importance to any analysis of the formation of rightist movements and to the role of the school in identity formation. Many writers have talked about the school as a productive site. It is a site for the production of student identities and for the production of a politics of identity formation.[42] Yet, other kind of identities are produced in interaction with state agencies such as schools. Oppositional identities centered around conservative cultural politics are formed as well. This is clear in the instance—one of many we expect—that we have investigated here.

The subject positions made available by the state were only two: "responsible" parents who basically supported "professional decision making," or "irresponsible" right-wing censors. The construction of this binary opposition created a situation in which the only ways parents and other community members could be *heard* was to occupy the spaces provided by the state. These were expanded and partly transformed, of course. But the only way for these concerned individuals to gain attention was for them to become increasingly aggressive about their claims and increasingly organized around conservative cultural and religious themes. Social identities are formed in this way. Thus, moderately conservative and "moderate" community members are slowly transformed into something very different. The Right *becomes* the Right in a complex and dynamic set of interactions with the state.[43]

At the outset of this analysis, we drew on the arguments of Whitty, Edwards, and Gewirtz: arguments in which they claim that the Right grows through "accidents." It grows in halting, diffuse, and partly indeterminate ways that are located in an entire complex of economic, political, and cultural relations. We shall miss much of this dynamic complexity if we focus only on conservative movements from the outside. Instead, we need to examine the situations within which they are built. We have suggested that a primary actor here is the bureaucratic state, which may have expanded its policing functions over knowledge for good reasons but which responds in ways that increase the potential for rightist movements to grow.

One thing became clear during this study. The linkages between parents who challenge textbooks and national "authoritarian populist" groups, grow during a controversy and as a result of such a controversy, rather than being forged by outside groups. In the case we have related here, a striking change is evident. A number of CCCV parents not only have become part of a larger network of New Right activists, but are proud of making such connections, connections that would have seemed to them to be impossible before. Here we need to stress again that these are individuals who had no prior links with New Right organizations and had no desire to be connected with such conservative groups until well into the *Impressions* controversy. Equally important is the fact that these newly formed links are continuing to grow stronger as new conservative political identities—extensions of the subject positions originally offered by the local state—are taken on by these people.

Economic conservativism and populism become linked to religious fundamentalism in these local ways. "Concerned citizens," upset by what the schools have defined as official knowledge and (correctly) worried about both the downward economic mobility of their children and the values that they are being taught, put these two forms of conservatism together not through any natural process, but in a manner that places the "knowledge policing" aspects of the state at the center of the formation of social allegiances and social movements.

Our points are not meant to imply that everyone has "free agency," that people "freely choose" to become Right (or anything else) in a vacuum. Indeed, exactly the opposite is the case. The increasing dominance of conservative positions on the entire range of issues involving education, the economy, sexuality, welfare, "intelligence,"[44] and so on—in the media and in public discussions—means that people in cities such as Citrus Valley and elsewhere live in a world where rightist discourses constantly circulate. It is now increasingly hard *not* to hear such interpretations, and even harder to hear positions opposed to them. However, there are multiple ways in which such discourses can be heard or read. Acceptance is but one of them.[45]

## DOES IT HAVE TO BE THIS WAY?

One is left here with many questions. But among the most important is this: Could it have been *different*? If the schools had listened more carefully, had not positioned the parents as censorious right wingers, would there have been a more progressive result? This is not "simply" a question about research. Given the Right's hegemonic project and the success of its ideological transformations, if schools are one of the crucial sites where these transformations occur, then interruptions of the bureaucratic gaze of the school and concrete struggles at a local level may be more important than we realize, not only in the short term but the long term as well. [46] In fact, it is just as crucial that schools focus their critical gaze on themselves and on how *they* may participate in creating the conditions in which ordinary citizens "become Right."

Fears about a declining economy or concerns about what is taught to one's children do not necessarily need to be sutured into an authoritarian populist attack on the state, nor do they necessarily have to be connected to the entire range of issues the Right stands for. Moderate and moderately traditional positions may not be ones all of our readers believe in, but there is a world of difference between such positions and the aggressive campaign against all that is public—and on the very idea of a truly public school—that emanates from the far right. The widespread effects of such groups can be limited only if the larger number of the public who have populist concerns about schools are not pushed to the right.

There is evidence that a different response to the politics of official knowledge by schools can have very different results, and it is worthwhile noting the experiences of schools that deal with such possibly polarizing situations in more open ways. [47] To take but one example, Fratney Street School in Milwaukee—a city that has suffered severely from the downturn in manufacturing jobs and from very real class and race antagonisms—faced a situation where political conflicts around class and racial dynamics could have provided quite fertile ground for the growth of rightist sentiments.

In Fratney Street School, which is situated in a "border area" in which its student population was one-third working class European Americans, one-third African American, and one-third Latino/Latina, the issues of whose knowledge was represented in the texts, of what an appropriate pedagogy would be, and of whose voices within that tense and diverse makeup would be listened to could have been as divisive as those that surfaced in Citrus Valley. These issues could have been ripe for the development of movements similar to those found in the case we have analyzed here. Yet, they did not lead to such development and in fact led to the formation of cross-class and cross-race coalitions for more progressive curricula and teaching and widespread support for the school.

Partly, this was due to a group of teachers and administrators who—as a group—opened up the discussion of curricula and pedagogy to the multiple voices with a stake in the school, including parents, community activists, and students. Constant attention was paid to the multiplicity of perspectives—not, as often happens in many school districts, as a form of "public relations" that usually is largely a form of the "engineering of consent"—but as an ongoing and genuine attempt to relate both the content of the curriculum and the decisions over it to the lives of the people involved. Partly, it was the result of the immense amount of work done by the educators to publicly justify what they felt was best for students, in words and in a style that could not be interpreted as arrogant, elitist, or distant, and to listen sympathetically and carefully to the fears, concerns, and hopes of the various voices in the community. And, finally, it was due to a decidedly nonhierarchical set of beliefs about what happens both within the school and between the school and the wider community(ies) of which it is a part.

None of this guarantees that the Right's restorational project will be transformed. Situations and their causes are indeed partly "accidental." Yet, the experiences at Fratney Street School and at other schools speaks to a very different articulation between the local state and its population, and it speaks to the very real possibility of interrupting a number of the conditions that lead to the growth of rightist social movements. Thus, saying no is not enough. There is work to be done.

# CHAPTER 4

# *American Realities: Poverty, Economy, and Education*

## with Christopher Zenk

In the previous two chapters, most of the attention was devoted both to analyzing the cultural/ideological dynamics behind important elements of the conservative alliance and to investigating some of the most crucial political conditions that lead to its growth at a local level. Yet cultural and political arguments are not sufficient to understand such growth. As Anita Oliver and I demonstrated in Chapter 3, in Citrus Valley and in so many communities across the country, economic fears—fears based on accurate intuitions about what is happening in this economy and on a partial understanding of the differential pattern of benefits that emerges from our economy—provide fertile ground for the emergence of restorational politics. Neoliberals are very good at using the discourse of economic crisis to bring this about. They have circulated a particular picture of this crisis, however. In this picture, schools sit center stage both as the institutions that deserve the lion's share of the blame for economic problems and as institutions that will fix nearly all that is wrong. Thus, a hegemonic alliance aimed at radically shifting education to the right can be created, if large numbers of people can be convinced that education is the primary cause of our economic problems and educational reform the universal panacea.

In this chapter, Christopher Zenk and I want to challenge the presuppositions about schools and the economy and the supposed connections between the two that lie behind the neoliberal emphasis on "education and jobs." It is not as useful to talk about this in general, however. Thus, we shall bring together a good deal of economic data to provide a very different picture from that provided by neoliberals. We shall use the issue of dropouts and "at risk" students as a way of entering into this debate.

## TAKING THE ECONOMY SERIOUSLY

It is almost impossible to pick up an issue of the most popular journals in education, to read our daily newspapers, or to listen to the statements made by federal, state, and local education officials without being confronted with the daily problems of struggling elementary and high school students. The issues range from high school dropout rates, to literacy rates, to shriveling math and science test scores, to privatizing failing schools, to diagnosing, labeling, and often even drugging students so they can make it through the school day. The problems appear endless, and popular understandings of them allow us to believe that every such "problem" begins in and is contained within the struggling students themselves; every "problem" also has immediate, direct, and implicitly detrimental economic implications.

Take the issue of high school dropout rates, which are always high among low-income populations, and especially so among poor people of color who are "at risk."[1] For many school and elected officials, especially those who are worried about our country's economic future, the usual chain of thinking about the high school dropout problem goes something like the following: If students didn't drop out there would be almost no unemployment and poverty in our inner cities. Better paying and more fulfilling jobs would await students upon graduation. The country as a whole would recover its economic productivity and competitiveness. Finally, the norms and skills the students would learn in school would prepare them to be productive and responsible citizens in the rosy economic future that would result. If we solve the dropout problem in schools, we will go a long way toward solving the social and economic problems in local communities. Fix the educational system and we will fix just about everything else. "Fix" the failing students and the floundering teachers and the "liberal" curriculum, and the nation will experience unprecedented economic well-being. So goes much of the accepted litany.

The dominant approach to understanding, analyzing, and addressing the concerns of schools involves the use of a *pathological* analysis; that is, the difficulties students and teachers face are perceived and described as existing within and caused primarily by "deficits" or "diseases" in the students themselves. So many of the criticisms of our educational system are based on this approach that we may be in danger of losing the ability to locate these issues in a more critical appraisal of their larger political and economic contexts.

Let us use the high school dropout rate as an example. While placing the spotlight on school dropouts is not totally a form of "educational hype," the insistent focus on this as largely (and often only) an educational problem—one that can be solved by small increments in funding, relatively minor changes in educational policies and practices, or limited programs of business and school "cooperation"—can lead us ultimately to misperceive the depth of the issue. It also can make it nearly inconceivable for us to generate policies in the larger social arena that will allow the hard work of educators and others to actually have an impact on students' lives.

Our aim here is to emphasize the fact that focusing on the issue of dropouts and "at risk" students as primarily an educational problem, and thus one that has primarily an educational solution, is *not* part of the solution but is itself a large part of the problem of cultural and economic disenfranchisement. We must cease framing the question of how to respond to educational failures—and high school dropouts, in particular—so that the only solutions (in the form of teachers' practices, students' achievement, and legislators' policies) either entirely blame or completely credit the students, the teachers, and the schools for outcomes like dropout rates. Given such a short-sighted perspective, it takes just a single causal step to see the failures of students, teachers, and schools as the roots of any economic downturn. Our goal is to problematize the popular understanding of where the primary responsibility for perpetuating—and interrupting—the cycle of school failure and poverty resides.

The assumption that we will find long-term answers to the dropout dilemma and to the realities of poverty and unemployment by keeping our attention within the school, is dangerously naive. Lasting answers will require a much more searching set of economic, social, and political questions and a considerably more extensive restructuring of our social commitments. Further, these will need to be accompanied by the democratization of our accepted ways of distributing and controlling jobs, benefits, education, and power. Until we take these larger economic and social contexts as seriously as they deserve, we shall simply be unable to respond adequately to the needs of youth in this country, beyond providing an endless series of short-lived placebos. In the process, we enable the Right to set the terms of the debate over education and over all things social. In order to more fully understand this, we shall need to examine what these contexts actually look like.

## AMERICAN REALITIES

Behind the rhetoric of economic recovery and sustainable, widespread economic growth is another reality. This is a reality of crisis, of an economy that increases the gap between rich and poor, between black and brown and red and yellow and white. It is driven by a set of policies in which the real lives of millions of people count less than "competitiveness," "efficiency," and above all profit maximization. Legitimating these policies is the jargon of economic "democracy," where social commitments and human relationships are judged solely by their marketplace achievements. Here, as was noted earlier, decisions of "democracy" are increasingly informed by and often completely conflated with the rules of capitalism and consumption. We live in a time when economic concentration is increasing, when the corporate sector takes on ever increasing power in our economic, political, and cultural lives. We live in a time when communities regularly trade needed tax bases derived from the income local corporations earn—taxes used for basic municipal and social services like schools, roads, and sewers—for low-wage, no-benefit jobs and wealthy, absentee conglomerate owners. While this may help the affluent, many commentators have raised serious doubts about its effects on those who historically have been less well served by our political and economic structures.

Carnoy, Shearer, and Rumberger put it this way: "Adam Smith notwithstanding, profit maximization by large, economically powerful, private corporations has not maximized the public good." The investment and employment decisions made by business have in large part generated "dislocation, discrimination, declining real wages, high unemployment, pollution, poor transportation systems, and run down crime-ridden cities."[2] These are not costed out when the corporate sector makes these decisions, but these social costs are borne by the public. The effects on communities, on the health and welfare of the bulk of the population, and on our cultural lives and education have been enormous.[3]

For those citizens and educators interested in working on a set of policies and practices that would have more democratic outcomes than these, one of the first steps is to gain a more adequate picture of the reality of this crisis. To do this, it is essential that we focus directly on the economy, rather than assuming that any such focus is somehow reductive and hence should be avoided. Other national leaders, educators, and industrialists have, of course, urged us to do the same thing, but with democratically suspect intentions. In report after report, we are told that we must make clearer linkages between schooling and the economy. The reason any unemployment exists, that workers—and particularly already suffering populations of workers—are poorly motivated, and that the United States increasingly fails to compete in the international economic arena, is that schools are failing. Or at the very least they aren't teaching the work skills and the ''basics'' they would be if they were as closely connected to economic priorities as they should be. Schools, according to this line of argument, have become inefficient and lead nowhere. Naturally, ''at risk'' students drop out. And the cycle continues.

As was argued earlier, the conservative and neoconservative positions that stand behind these calls for redefining the goals of the educational system into those primarily of industry and the Right simply act to export the crisis in the economy onto the schools.[4] Here, we want to look more directly at what the current and future economy seems to have in store for us. No serious discussion of educational concerns in general and of dropouts specifically can go on unless we situate these issues within what is happening outside the school. In a relatively brief chapter, it will not be possible to deal with all aspects of our economy. What we shall do here is select certain aspects that tend to highlight the current and future prospects of the paid labor market. We shall pay particular attention to the structures of poverty in the United States and to the emerging trends in job loss and job creation in the economy. In the process, we want to focus on some of the class, race, and gender dynamics that have played such a major role in structuring opportunities for the educational achievement of youth and for youth employment. Finally, we want to relate some of the experiences that many youth have on the job, experiences that should make us question our notions of success.

In a series of previous studies, a picture of the structure of inequalities in American society has been drawn. Let us update and summarize these findings.[5]

Between 1967 and 1992 the share of aggregate household income for the highest 20% of American households grew steadily, rising from 43.8% to 46.9%. Over the same span, the income share of the middle 60% of households decreased from 52.3% to 49.4%, and the share of the lowest 20% of households dropped from 4.0% to 3.8%. Thus, by 1992 four-fifths of the U.S. population was earning just over half of the nation's total income.[6] One might say that over the past 3 decades 80% of our country's population has handed over an ever increasing proportion of their earnings to an already unreasonably wealthy minority.

If we consider race in an analysis of income distribution, and at the same time specify the income dollar amounts behind these income distribution percentages, the extent of this reallocation of wealth becomes truly disturbing. Since 1967, the mean income of the top 5% of white families has grown by 38%, to an average of over $160,000 per year. Over the same period the mean income for the poorest one-fifth of black families has shrunk 21%, to a 1992 mean family income of $4,255 per year. Simple division shows that the richest white families in the United States have gone from earning around 20 times what our poorest black families were bringing home nearly 30 years ago, to earning nearly 40 times what these same black families garnered in 1992.[7] These figures, even if taken by themselves, indicate a marked, continual, and growing redistribution of income and benefits from the poor to the rich.[8] They are made even more significant by the fact that the middle class itself may actually be shrinking as the numbers at the extremes grow. We have more and more a "double peaked" economic distribution as the numbers of well to do and poor increase.

These inequalities—though growing—have been around for quite some time. In the United States, the bottom 20% of the population receives a smaller percentage of total after-tax income than the comparable groups in Japan, Sweden, Australia, Norway, the Netherlands, France, West Germany, the United Kingdom, and a number of other nations. In fact, our lowest 20% of the population earns less than half the total percentage of after-tax income earned by the lowest 20% of the Japanese population.[9] Additionally, in a comparison of these same countries, the top 10% of the population of the United States garners the highest percentage of our respective total national income—a phenomenal 28.2%.[10] And the top 20% of the U.S. population receives an astronomical 42% of the total national household income, a number significantly higher than in all of the countries mentioned above except France.[11] The amount of money represented by these statistics is vast and is certainly indicative of a trend heavily favoring the top 20% of the U.S. and Western world population.

Recent analysis of the relationship between youth income and high school dropout rates, completed by the National Center for Education Statistics, provides a quick glimpse of what income means for school completion. The poorest 20% of youths ages 16 to 24 were more than 10 times more likely to drop out of high school than the wealthiest 20% of youths—evidenced by a comparison of the groups' 24.6% and 2.3% dropout rates.[12] And the poorest black youths were 30 times more likely to drop out of high school than were the wealthiest black youths.[13]

Yet this is not all. One out of every seven Americans lives in poverty,[14] as does one out of every four children under the age of 6.[15] And nearly one in three Americans will have been poor at some point in their lives by the time they reach 16[16]—just about the time when dropping out of school and finding a job looks like the surest way out of poverty, or when staying in school appears to be academically impractical, offering no opportunity for short-term success and even less of a chance of long-term benefits. Based on statistics from just the past 10 years, these numbers are growing, as we shall indicate later.

Nearly 30% of all Hispanics and one-third of all African Americans live below the poverty line.[17] In 1992 almost 30% of families living below the poverty line received no food stamps, Medicaid, housing subsidies, or low-price school lunches, while only around 42% received cash assistance through such programs as Aid to Families with Dependent Children.[18] Even the government has estimated that the diet of those living at the official poverty level is so deficient "that it is suitable only for 'temporary or emergency use.'"[19] And in an age when welfare programs are under attack as "free rides" for a "lazy" poor, it is especially poignant to note that poor children's families earn twice as much money from work as they receive from welfare assistance.[20]

It is difficult not to ask at this point about the direct impact of child poverty on school attendance and achievement, on high school dropout rates, on the future earning potential of individuals, and on the general economic well-being of the nation. *Wasting America's Future*, a report on the costs of child poverty recently published by the Children's Defense Fund, provides the answers to such inquiries, in all too unsettling terms. Overall, youths who experience poverty during childhood are more than 300% more likely to never finish high school than children who never experience poverty.[21] For every year that we tolerate the current child poverty level, our nation suffers an estimated $36 to $177 billion in reduced future worker productivity and employment.[22] And the estimated bottom-line results of ending just one year of child poverty range from a net cost of $10 billion to a potential net gain of $131 billion.[23]

These "bottom lines" are not the only effects of child poverty, though. And they do not provide an accurate picture of the difficulties involved in addressing child poverty in the United States. Marian

Wright Edelman articulates the complexity of the child poverty/future opportunities relationship.

> Child poverty stalks its survivors down every avenue of their lives. It places them at greater risk of hunger, homelessness, sickness, physical or mental disability, violence, educational failure, teen parenthood, and family stress, and deprives them of positive early childhood experiences and the adolescent stimulation and creative outlets that help prepare more affluent children for school and then college and work. . . . The worst of it is, poverty doesn't trigger just one or two or even 10 discrete problems that can be easily isolated and addressed. Many poverty-related problems and deficits interact and combine with each other in a unique way for every child, so we cannot make real headway against the effects of poverty by tackling them one at a time. . . . It is a miracle that the great majority of poor children stay in school, do not commit crimes, and strive to be productive citizens in a society that guarantees them a prison bed if they fail (for over $30,000 a year) but refuses to provide them a Head Start (for less than $3,800 a year) or a summer job (for less than $1,400) to help them succeed. [24]

The living and health conditions of poor children—and the potential impact of these conditions on academic success and school completion—also are infrequently considered. Poor children are nearly four times as likely as nonpoor children to live among signs of rats and mice, and nearly three times as likely to live in a house that is "too cold" for 24 hours or more in the winter. [25] Poor children face a significantly higher chance (as high as four times that of nonpoor children) of being classified as mildly mentally retarded, of having physical or mental disabilities, of being hospitalized for injuries, of having iron deficiencies, and of missing school due to chronic and acute health conditions. [26] Low-income children average nine points lower on IQ tests given at age 5, and are 1.3 times more likely to have learning disabilities. And each year of childhood spent in poverty results in an increased likelihood that a child will be below the usual school grade level for her or his age. [27]

It is impossible to consider the existence of such levels of child poverty—and the basic health and educational inequalities that they cause—as "unavoidable" outgrowths of our economic system, or as necessary evils we trade for general economic well-being. These levels of child poverty are a uniquely American phenomenon. American children are twice as likely to be poor as Canadian children, three times as likely to be poor as British children, four times as likely to be poor as French children, and seven to thirteen times more likely to be poor than Swedish, Dutch, and German children.[28] Isn't it ironic that a nation that proclaims as one of its primary goals of family life and formal schooling the teaching of "values" does so much less than its industrialized peers to protect children and families against poverty?[29]

The poverty rate is basically an indicator of the state of the economy.[30] The effects of the deteriorating economic conditions of the past 15 years are clearly visible in the fact that since 1980—or essentially since Ronald Reagan was elected to the White House—the "pretransfer poverty" rate (that is, the poverty rate before including government assistance) has not fallen below 20%, and in 1992 was nearly 23%.[31] For blacks and Hispanics these rates remained near or above 40% in 1992.[32] In the same period, even when we factor in all transfer payments, the poverty rate climbed from approximately 11% to well over 15% and, although it has fluctuated mildly in recent years, it again hovers near 15%.[33] Much of this effect was the result of the decline in the economy and, just as important, in the steady erosion in the value of the transfers poor people received.[34] Put simply, while the poverty rate did show a real decline from 1959 to 1969 and showed some modest progress until 1978, it turned up sharply in the 1980s[35] and has remained high in the 1990s.[36] Rather than getting better, for those on the bottom it is getting much worse. This may be accepted by many Americans because of the Right's increasing ability to create a more selfish society, one in which our sense of the common good has begun to whither.[37]

Gary Burtless paints a less than sanguine picture of this situation.

> In view of America's deep seated beliefs, there are scant grounds for optimism that the lot of this nation's poor will soon be radically improved. The steep rise in social welfare spending between 1960 and 1980 substantially raised the well-being of many poor families, and these improvements ought not be lightly dismissed. But much of the increased spending was concentrated on the lucky poor insured by our social insurance programs—the aged, the infirm, and the insured unemployed. . . . In the recent past, government initiative to reduce poverty has come to a halt and may even have been reversed.[38]

Gender, race, and age inequalities also are so pervasive as to be almost painful to recount. In 1992, women working year-round and full-time still earned only just over two-thirds of what men in the same category earned, up only a few percentage points from a decade earlier.[39] And looking at the median income of individuals in 1992 (arguably a statistic that better reflects the income of the average worker in the United States, because its primary relation is to the population of earners rather than to the combined income dollar totals of all individuals), we find that black males earned just 59% of the median income for white males, while Hispanic males received just 64% of this same total. Even worse, white females earned 51%, Hispanic females just 41%, and black females a minuscule 39% of the median white male income. [40]

And if these income differentials aren't distressing enough we can look more closely at the *intersections* of income, race, gender, and poverty. In 1992, the median income of black and Hispanic female householders[41] (i.e., women who head a family without a husband present) was more than $1,000 below the poverty line income for families of four or more members. [42] Between 1980 and 1993 the percentage of black families earning less than $5,000 per year actually jumped by 50%, to an astonishing 11.3%. [43] More than a decade later not only were more black families in poverty, but more black families were falling farther and farther below the official poverty income level, already an arbitrary and ludicrously low figure. For, as commissions in Idaho and New Hampshire determined, a federal poverty line income is between 17% and 29% below a minimal budget for a family of four. [44] Given these analyses and averages, severely limited public assistance programs that supplement a family's income in an attempt to raise it to a poverty level or sustenance level income become not only less and less effective but so massively insufficient as to be nearly practically and economically irrelevant.

As of 1992 women still required a college degree in order to equal the median earnings of men with just high school diplomas. [45] For year-round, full-time workers 25 years and older, the second largest disparity in income between the sexes exists between those women and men with no high school diploma (the largest is between professionally degreed women and men). [46] In 1981, nearly 53% of the families headed by black women and over 27% of those headed by white women were officially poor; by 1992 these rates had jumped to 60.4% for blacks and 40.3% for whites. [47] If we consider the elderly poor, 71% are women[48] and, in 1992, of the elderly black women living alone, 86% were defined as pretransfer poor. [49] Overall, black and brown men and women earn less than two-thirds the income of whites; even those black and Latino men and women pursuing higher levels of formal education—all the way through masters degrees—earn only around 80% of the income of whites with comparable education. [50] Nearly 40% (73% for 18- to 24-year-olds) of black men and 42% of Hispanic men (68% for 18- to 24-year-olds) were officially classified as workers with "low annual earnings" in 1989.[51] And access to comparable jobs is just about blocked and seems to be worsening given current economic conditions and policies.

Finally, examining unemployment makes the picture of this part of our economy even more graphic. Some econometric measures indicate that the unequal cumulative impact of unemployment on minorities and women actually doubled between 1951 and 1981. The data on unemployment rates tell a similar story. Although the current figures of 12.9% for blacks and 6.0% for whites are lower than the 21% and 9.7% rates in 1982, the differential has not lessened.[52] For white teenagers, the unemployment rate in 1993 was 16.2%; for Hispanic youths, a dramatically higher 26.2%; and for black youths, a staggering 38.9%, and even higher in many urban areas.[53] For these and other reasons, the income gap between white and black families continues to widen at an ever increasing rate.

THE CURRENT STRUCTURING OF PAID EMPLOYMENT

The issue of unemployment is of considerable importance here and needs further discussion, especially its relation to the racial and sexual divisions in American society that we just described. Certain trends are truly disturbing.

The historical changes are striking. While labor force participation of white men declined from 82% in 1940 to 76% in 1980 and has remained steady since (in large part because of a drop in participation by white men over the age of 55), for black men the story is dramatically different. In 1940, 84% were in the paid labor force. By 1980, only 67% participated in the labor force. The figures become even more graphic if we increase the time span. In 1930, 80% of all black men were employed; by 1983 this had fallen to 56%. In 1993 this percentage had risen only to the 67% range.[54] This, of course, has connections to the transformation of agricultural labor in the United States. The decline was particularly steep for blacks aged 24 or younger.[55] Already dangerously low, the labor force participation rate for black men under the age of 20 refuses to stabilize.[56]

Though bad enough, this does not tell the entire story. We also must discuss the skyrocketing rates of mortality and the causes of death among black men. In 1991 the "expected death" rate for 20-year-old black men was nearly double that of similarly aged white men, 1.39 per 1,000 versus 2.74.[57] During the Reagan/Bush years

(1980–1992), this rate jumped 30% for young black men, while dropping 26% for young white men.[58] And these deaths are also increasingly violent ones for young black men. Violent and accidental deaths for black men aged 15 to 24 increased by 43% in the 1980s;[59] for white men of the same age over the same span the death rate from violence and accidents fell by nearly 25%.[60] An even closer look reveals that black boys of high school age die at the end of firearms almost five times more frequently than do white boys in the same age range.[61] Given overall death rates for youths of high school age and the differential between these rates for black and white males, one might even argue that the reason young black men aren't graduating from high school is because they aren't living long enough to do so.

The rising rates of incarceration for black and brown men, and especially juveniles, are also alarming and revealing. Of course, we need to frame any discussion of rates of imprisonment in the United States with one racial breakdown, that of the general population. In 1992 Latinos/Latinas and blacks made up only 16% of the population of the United States, while whites accounted for more than 80%.[62] Compare these numbers to 1991 statistics that show that 58.8% of jail inmates,[63] 64.7% of state prison inmates,[64] and 35% of federal prisoners were people of color.[65] While the overall percentage of juveniles held in public facilities increased by 5% between 1987 and 1989, the percentage of "minority" juveniles in such facilities increased by 13% (14% for blacks and 10% for Hispanics), while the percentage of nonminority juveniles actually decreased by 5%.[66] On December 31, 1991, a total of 395,245 black prisoners were under the jurisdiction of state and federal correctional authorities in the United States, while only 385,347 whites were.[67] Blacks are more than five times more likely than whites to be in the custody of correctional authorities, and black men are nearly eight times as likely as white men to be murdered or killed by law enforcement officers.[68] Based on these numbers, it is clear that the United States seems to have decided to deal with poverty by jailing or allowing to die a large percentage of people of color, many of whose crimes and needs are directly related to the economic and housing conditions and the patterns of racial segregation they experience. This has had a dramatic impact on family structure and on the sense of a future among black youth.

In the early 1980s the Center for the Study of Social Policy projected that if then-current economic trends continued, by the end of this century we would witness 70% of all black families headed by single women. Analysis of 1993 statistics shows us to be solidly on track for a 60% rate by the year 2000,[69] but already nearly 70% of

black children are born to unmarried women.[70] This condition is best
stated by Ellwood and Summers in their discussion of the employment possibilities of black youth: "By every conceivable measure the
labor market situation for young blacks is bad and getting worse." As
they go on to say, "The magnitude of the problem cannot be over-
stated: in 1980, before the recession exerted a major effect, only one
out-of-school black youth in three had any job."[71] Today's figures are
no better.

Once people of color are hired, moreover, their rates of advancement continue to be slower. They are also considerably more vulnera-
ble to job loss during periods of economic retrenchment. The supposedly booming "new" service economy has not changed this situation
in any appreciable way. The paid employment patterns show the
usual positions: the secondary labor market dominated by low paying
jobs, many of which are less than full time, with little or no benefits,
little job security, and no unions.[72]

This highlights an important point. Unemployment rates are differentiated by type of paid job. In all Western countries, manual
and "unskilled" workers suffer much greater unemployment than
professional and nonmanual occupations. Sex and race play a major
part here, as do the international division of labor and what is called
capital flight, referring to the practice of companies that shift their
plants from country to country seeking cheaper and nonunionized
workers in the Third World. Any analysis of the effects of NAFTA and
GATT will show that these "agreements" have only accelerated this
abandonment of U.S. workers for nations where workers can be more
easily exploited.[73] Women's paid work is also concentrated in the
secondary labor market in the same way as minority paid employment. In 1993 women accounted for 61.7% of workers in service industries,[74] where the average salary is frequently the lowest of all
U.S. industries and where benefits are minimal at best.[75] In fact, in
most Western industrialized nations the unemployment rate is lower
for men than for women, often dramatically so.[76] And these differences actually may be understated since "the discouraged worker
effect" tends to have a greater impact on women, especially in times
of economic decline.[77]

One last and increasingly significant element in this situation
needs to be noted, especially since it bears heavily on the issue of
dropouts. Since 1973, a particular feature of unemployment has been
growing. This is the disproportionate effect of unemployment on
potential young workers. In the United States, the youth (ages 16–
19) unemployment rate in 1993 was 19.0%, while the rate for all

workers was 6.8%.[78] As noted earlier in this chapter, unemployment rates for youths in the United States were at least double and up to six times the overall employment rate, depending on race. Of course, one might look at the conspicuous overall 24.3% unemployment rate for high school dropouts in the United States and argue that such a number bears out the argument that our youth would escape their dismal economic futures if only they stayed in school. But this number is actually *lower* than the 26.8% of 16- to 24-year-old blacks who had finished high school and were unemployed.[79] This presents a major ideological as well as economic problem. For a substantial portion of the new generation of youth, what is being offered is a future with no long-term prospect of earning a living outside of meager welfare benefits. "Neither diligence and discipline, nor mass consumption, are likely to rise out of that experience."[80] The concentration of unemployment among the young has not been seen in previous economic crises, but now has seemingly become a norm of our economic system rather than a signal that a larger, foundational crisis exists. And yet, as much of a structural commonplace as high youth unemployment has become, popular appraisals of the roots of any of our economic woes quickly locate the cause in the children or the schools. The social consequences of this normalization undoubtedly will be with us for years to come.[81]

Thus, it is clear that the burden of unemployment falls unequally across age, race, and sex groups. Persons of color, women, and the young are the most affected.[82] These groups dominate the lowest paid and least autonomous positions in the economy, primarily those in the service industry.[83] In 1989 women represented 80% of all administrative support positions, but only 9% of precision production, craft, and repair workers. Women held 68% of all retail and personal service sales positions, but only 40% of executive, managerial, and administrative jobs.[84] And in 1990, women, people of color, and youths were on average twice as likely to have "low annual earnings" (an hourly rate of $6.10 or below) as white men.[85] These obvious ways in which our economy creates divisions in employment and unemployment—and contributes to the generation and exacerbation of social tensions—should give us pause.

These unemployment statistics are very deceptive, however. The measured unemployment rate does not capture the severity of the problem. It does not reflect alterations in the duration of joblessness. Some surveys in Western capitalist nations have documented that the average length of unemployment rose from 7 weeks in 1970 to over 45 weeks in 1984. And between 1980 and 1993 the percentage of

workers in the United States experiencing longer than 6-month unemployment periods nearly doubled, while the overall unemployment duration for all unemployed persons increased by more than
50%, from an average of 11.9 weeks to 18.1 weeks.[86] And this average
was almost 10% longer for blacks than for whites.[87] Thus, most often
these statistics on unemployment refer to people who are still unemployed and "relate only to their current period of unemployment."[88]

Just as significant, the usual measures of unemployment do not
register what has been called the hidden unemployed, those people
who have become so discouraged by the constant negative experiences of finding only part-time, temporary, or low-wage jobs, or no
jobs at all, that they no longer actively seek paid work. It is not
unusual to find nearly as many individuals in these categories as in
the official unemployment statistics.[89] If these categories were included, so that we had an accurate picture of what was really going
on, we would come close, at a minimum, to doubling the official
rates.

Yet, even all of the foregoing figures do not tell the whole story.
As we noted above, the differential rates and kinds of employment
between men and women and between whites and people of color,
make it clear that the sexual and racial divisions of labor structure the
experiences of groups of people in markedly different ways.

Finally, simply considering numbers of paid workers does not
tell us what changes have occurred in the kinds of work people do.
For instance, working as a janitor making minimum wage is qualita-
tively different from working in a steel mill for $15.00 an hour. Both
are employment. But the type of job, the rate of pay, the social relations on the job, the autonomy, the respect, and so on, are radically
different. The lowering of the official unemployment rate may hide
what is really going on in truly significant ways.

THE FUTURE ECONOMY

The previous section gave an indication of what the economy
and the paid labor market now looks like if we reposition ourselves
and look at it not from the top down but from the bottom up, from
the perspective of women, people of color, and youth. (It is important
again to state that these groups are not, of course, mutually exclusive.) Given this present structure, what does the future hold in store
in terms of the paid labor market for youth who will make decisions
about their schooling?

We need, of course, to be very careful about generalizing too readily from the economic data we shall review in this section. We are reminded of two rather biting lines about economists: "If all economists were laid end to end, they would still not reach a conclusion" and "An economist is an expert who will know tomorrow why the things he predicted yesterday didn't happen today."[90] Even with these cautions, however, there are certain tendencies that can be seen. Among the most important for discussions about dropouts and "at risk" youth are the long-term trends in job loss and job creation. Those trends first became apparent over a decade ago, but have become well-established norms since.

In the manufacturing sector, approximately 600,000 jobs are expected to be lost between the years 1990 and 2005.[91] Technological changes and pressures to increase productivity, while limiting employment and lowering wages, will limit job expansion. It is in the service sector that most new positions will be found. This sector broadly includes personal care, home health aides, social workers, hotel and lodging workers, restaurant employees, transportation workers, business services, and other services. It is projected to account for fully 95% of all new jobs created between 1990 and 2005.[92] These so-called "other services" will continue to grow the fastest in the next decade and a half. Health and business services alone will provide one out of every four new jobs.[93]

The Bureau of Labor Statistics develops projections for 1,500 individual occupations. The top ten are shown in the Table 4.1 and are projected to account for one-fourth of the total employment change in the United States for the period 1992–2005.[94]

The top eight of these ten occupations—retail salespersons, cashiers, office clerks, truck drivers, waitresses/waiters, nursing aides/orderlies, food preparation workers, and janitors—in general do not require high levels of education.[95] The ten occupations with the fastest growth rates during the period most often are linked to the emerging technological restructuring of parts of our economy or to medical services. Table 4.2 documents these trends.[96]

The majority of the occupations just mentioned require a fair amount of skill and training and do signify a slowly growing emergence of a technically sophisticated sector of the paid labor market. Yet, with this said, it is of great importance that we examine Table 4.2 carefully. For while the fastest growth rates occur in these occupations, taken together they constitute only one-fifth of the total employment growth in the entire nation.[97] Thus, the comparison leads to a less sanguine understanding of where the bulk of the paid em-

**Table 4.1.** *Civilian employment in occupations with largest job growth: 1992–2005 (in millions of jobs, with moderate projections).*

| Occupation | 1992 | 2005 | % |
|---|---|---|---|
| Salespersons, retail | 3.7 | 4.4 | +21.5 |
| Registered nurses | 1.8 | 2.6 | +41.7 |
| Cashiers | 2.7 | 3.4 | +24.4 |
| General office clerks | 2.7 | 3.3 | +24.3 |
| Truck drivers | 2.3 | 3.0 | +27.1 |
| Waiters/waitresses | 1.8 | 2.4 | +36.3 |
| Nursing aides, orderlies, attendants | 1.3 | 1.9 | +45.4 |
| Janitors/cleaners | 2.9 | 3.4 | +19.1 |
| Food preparation workers | 1.2 | 1.7 | +45.1 |
| Systems analysts | .5 | 1.0 | +120 |

**Table 4.2.** *Civilian employment in the fastest growing occupations: 1992–2005 (in thousands, with moderate projections).*

| Fastest Growing | 1992 | 2005 | #Change | % Change |
|---|---|---|---|---|
| Home health aides | 287 | 550 | 263 | 91.7 |
| Paralegals | 90 | 167 | 77 | 85.2 |
| Systems analysts/ computer scientists | 463 | 829 | 366 | 78.9 |
| Personal/home care aides | 103 | 183 | 80 | 76.7 |
| Physical therapists | 88 | 155 | 67 | 76 |
| Medical assistants | 165 | 287 | 122 | 73.9 |
| Operations research analysts | 57 | 100 | 42 | 73.2 |
| Human services workers | 145 | 249 | 103 | 71.2 |
| Radiologic technologists/ techicians | 149 | 252 | 103 | 69.5 |
| Medical secretaries | 232 | 390 | 158 | 68.3 |

ployment will be. Even with the relative rapidity of growth in high-tech-related jobs, the kinds of work that will be increasingly available to a large portion of the American population will not be highly skilled, technically elegant positions. Just the opposite will be the case. The labor market will be increasingly dominated by low paying, repetitive work in the retail trade and service sectors. This is made strikingly clear by one fact: There will be more cashier jobs created—approximately 700,000—by 2005 than jobs for computer scientists, systems analysts, physical therapists, operations analysts, and radiologic technicians *combined*.

Yet it is not only job creation and job loss in the lower paying areas of the service sector of the economy that will be of concern. The middle class itself has begun to feel the impact of these processes, something that will worsen in the future. One knowledgeable economist puts it this way.

> Just as employers have an economic incentive to fragment jobs into component parts in order to reduce labor costs, they also have an economic incentive to automate jobs that pay the highest wages. Thus expert systems and other sophisticated technologies are more likely to eliminate more skilled, high-salaried jobs than less-skilled, low salary ones. The increased use of these devices will create new jobs in industries where they are manufactured and new jobs related to their use and maintenance. But recent employment projections for the U.S. suggest that few new jobs will be created in these areas. [98]

Even those high-tech occupations that previously have required considerable skill—computer programming offers a good example—increasingly are being subject to deskilling, less autonomy, and lower pay. This may be related to the "feminization" of many of these jobs, as well as the tendency to mechanize and standardize them. [99] Unfortunately, given the power of patriarchal assumptions and relations in our society, the paid and unpaid labor of women historically has been subject to significant pressures of rationalization, proletarianization, loss of autonomy and control, and less respect. [100] Thus, other occupations that traditionally have been seen as largely "women's jobs" will be affected by the technological restructuring that is occurring. Clerical work, banking services, telecommunications, and so on will all see the effects of these processes of deskilling. [101]

Yet no discussion of what is happening to "women's work" is complete unless we seriously face an issue of critical import in any analysis of the economy. We need to remember that young women face the prospects of a dual labor market. They are trained for the paid labor market outside the home and for unpaid labor within the home. Too often, discussions of dropouts, youth employment and unemployment, and the economic structures surrounding the school, focus totally on paid work. This is a serious deficiency and vitiates much of the power of these analyses, since they cannot deal adequately with the realities that young women face every day not only in making decisions about schooling and paid work, but in structuring experiences of so much of their lives. These analyses, hence, tend all too often to be based on a lack of understanding of the importance, both in terms of identity and in terms of the economy, of the labor of caring that women do. The logic of these analyses may tacitly reflect patriarchal assumptions. While we cannot go into detail here about this, it is essential that we begin to understand more fully not only the effects of the political economy of capitalism on the lives and futures of youth, but the political economy of patriarchal relations as well. [102]

### EXPERIENCING PAID WORK

Given what we have shown here about what the future holds in store, it should be clear that a large portion of youth—especially those who are poor or working class, many young women, and persons of color—will find particular kinds of paid jobs. These jobs will tend to be concentrated in the secondary labor market. They will be characterized by and large by low pay, poor working conditions, few benefits, and an unskilled or deskilled labor process. [103] That is, of course, if these youth survive beyond high school age or are not incarcerated through their teens. One might want to question why they would rush to jobs like these in the first place or why they would see a relationship between schooling and the supposedly marvelous future of paid and unpaid work.

This issue is made more poignant in the comments—which are repeated time and again by others in similar circumstances—of young men and women who were able to find a path to a first paid job in the secondary sector. The deskilled nature of the paid jobs available can be seen in a quote from a young woman who after only 3 days on a clerical job already felt the burden of what her future work would look like.

> It was very boring and I [spent all] three days [doing] photocopying. It's not right, that they make one person do the same job all the time. I

should've been switched round with some of the others. I wouldn't want to do that for a job all the time. [104]

Another student put it even more graphically in describing a low paying building maintenance job he was finally placed in.

I was treated like slave labor. I hated it and left after a day. They were . . . telling me to do this and not doing it themselves, so I told 'em to fuck off and went home in the afternoon and didn't go back again. [105]

A final quote may illuminate the reality of these jobs.

I was cooking in kitchens and it was boring. You couldn't talk to the others much because they (machines) were organized in separate sections and you cooked in one section or another. It was stupid really. They didn't have to work it like that. They just did. [106]

What is interesting about these perceptions is that each of these individuals looked forward to leaving school and finally getting paid work. [107] Yet the experience of the job was so boring and often so demeaning that it was clear that the dream of finally becoming autonomous and getting the economic rewards associated with a paid job, was shattered by the reality of the workplace itself. In all these comments, one is reminded of John Masefield's lines:

> To get the whole world out of bed,
>     and washed, and dressed, and warmed, and fed,
>     to work, and back to bed again,
>     Believe me, Saul, costs worlds of pain. [108]

The future world of paid and unpaid work that so many of our students will face, the structures of inequality, and the realities of poverty that they will experience and that are growing should make us pay much closer attention to whether we can solve our educational problems without dealing with the root causes of our dilemmas. This is a point we want to highlight in our concluding section.

### PLACING THE BLAME WHERE IT BELONGS

To attack the schools for the decline of ''excellence'' and for the economic crisis is easy. But to deal with the processes that actually cause this situation is much harder. As we hinted at the end of the prior section, without dealing with the social causes of dropouts and the larger issue of educational differentiation in general, without taking seriously the historic dominance of structures of class, race, and gender stratification that are so fundamental a part of American society inside and outside the school, we will simply fail. [109]

We must resist the urge to place the blame on the educational system for the problems of our economic decline, for our lack of economic competitiveness, for unemployment, and so on. If we take two paradigm cases of industries that have declined over the past years—steel and automobile—their declines may be due much more to managerial failure and conscious decisions to deindustrialize than to things such as skill shortages. "These examples might lead to reforming business schools or investment practices" or to national economic policies that are considerably more democratic both in planning and outcomes, but one thing they do not provide is any consistent justification for blaming the school for the economic disarray we face. [110]

What are the reasons that educational restructuring is given so much importance in dealing with unemployment and underemployment? One reason is the government's need for legitimacy. It must *be seen* to be doing something about these problems. [111] Reforming education is not only widely acceptable and relatively unthreatening, but just as crucially, "its success or failure will not be obvious in the short-term." A second is what is partly a social Darwinist principle that distances the economy as a major cause of its own troubles: "The assertion that unemployment is due to the lack of skills of the labor force helps sustain a belief in the basic virtues of the economic system. If *only* the individual had studied harder, or was willing to take lower wages, the inequalities in society arising with unemployment could be eliminated!" [112]

Even though the American public "may find it reassuring to believe that poor children will enjoy the same economic prospects as everyone else if only they learn to read and do their sums, this reassuring belief is wrong." In fact, when one examines the instances where students from different economic backgrounds do equally well on such measures as widely used standardized tests, this supposed equality of achievement reduced the difference in the earnings they made as adults by only one-third. The issue then may not revolve as much around school achievement as around the socioeconomic relations and structures that organize society. [113]

It is quite possible, in fact, that the narrowing of school achievement differences between the poor and the nonpoor will make very little difference in terms of poverty or inequality. We may have a situation in which credential inflation creates what is known as a system of "queuing," in which advantaged groups maintain their own positions. The level of educational achievement and the credential that once may have qualified someone for a specific type of employment is "discounted." The credential needed for the job is raised, and the previously required achievement level is useful only to open the door to a lesser paying job. [114] The issue of dropping out needs to be considered in this light.

We will need to face the fact that economic disparities that are "based on race, sex and family headship are extremely difficult to reduce." This point will be returned to in the concluding chapter of this book. Although it is essential that we focus on those areas of our educational system that need to be restructured, securing answers to the problem of dropouts and students who are "at risk" will require more than short-term interventions such as limited training programs, counseling, and placement services. It requires long-term changes in the structure of labor markets, "in the provision of transitional income, employment, and in kind support." It involves expanding educational opportunities and large-scale and continued funding for such educational programs. Finally, and perhaps most important, it requires a growing economy that has meaningful jobs at the end of one's school experience. [115]

Whether this can be accomplished, given our current economic assumptions and given the conservative restoration, is questionable. But there are sets of progressive economic and social policies that have been articulated that could be more than a little helpful in moving us toward a more democratically controlled economy, polity, and educational system. In particular, the work of Nove; Carnoy, Shearer, and Rumberger; Raskin; and Simon, Dippo, and Schenke deserve much greater attention from educators concerned with the relationship between education and the economy. [116]

One transitional goal should be to add one more inalienable right to every American: the right to a decent and respectful job. [117] This would, of course, require both that we work toward a fundamental restructuring of our economic priorities and that we challenge the social Darwinist assumptions that stand behind so much of our economic system. (You know—They got poor or unemployed the old fashioned way. They earned it.) The poor and the under- and unemployed didn't "earn it." The shattering of their hopes and dreams; the disintegration of their families, communities, and educational institutions; the despair and struggles are a "gift" from our economy. This is one time a gift should be sent back, unopened.

As we have documented in this chapter, in confining our analysis of dropouts and "at risk" youth to the internal qualities of our educational system, we will miss the economic realities that surround the school and provide the present and future context in which our youth will function. It would not be an overstatement to say that our kind of economy—with its growing inequalities; its structuring of what are increasingly alienating, more deskilled, and meaningless jobs; its emphasis on profit no matter what the social cost—"naturally" *produces* the conditions that lead to dropping out, in much the same way that the lack of schooling, decent housing, and health care in the Asian nation with which this book began, was produced by cheap french fries. The phenomenon of the dropout is not an odd aberration that randomly arises in our school system. It is structurally generated, created out of the real and unequal relations of economic, political, and cultural resources and power that organize this society. Poverty is cyclical—and, yes, a very real relationship between education and economics does exist—but we must recognize that the origins of this cycle are in our social and economic relations, not in our schools. Solutions to high dropout rates and other examples of educational failure will require that we no longer hide from these realities. The first step is looking at our economy honestly and recognizing how the class, race, and gender relations that structure it operate.

What should guide us in dealing with these dilemmas is the political principle of the *common good*, not simply profit. This principle asserts that "no inhuman act should be used as a short cut to a better day" and that any program in education, in politics, in health and welfare, in the economy or elsewhere must be evaluated "against the likelihood that it will result in linking equity, sharing, personal dignity, security, freedom and caring."[118] The economic and social policies now in place, and especially those being instituted in this time of conservative triumphalism, fall well short of this. The result is untold misery for millions of people and a future that is more than a little bleak for many of the youth of this nation. Perhaps we could begin by asking ourselves a question that has a long history in the tradition of democratic movements in the United States: Whose side are you on?

CHAPTER 5

# Conclusion:
# Taking the Fun Out of
# Educational Reform

"Whose side are you on?" is a powerful, yet utterly complex, question. In order to take it seriously, this book had to be wide ranging. But, the book is anchored in an unromantic appraisal of the dangers a critical education faces in today's world. It is also anchored in personal experience: not only in my work in the Asian nation with which I began Chapter 1, but in the gritty memories of the years I spent teaching in poor neighborhoods and being president of a teachers' union that was trying to do something about the distressing educational conditions students and teachers in these areas faced every day.

When I began my career as an educator, my first teaching assignment was working in an all African American and Latino/Latina inner city school. We were instructed *not* to allow children ever to use "nonstandard English" or to speak Spanish. We were to actively intervene when this occurred. Our job was to turn "them" as quickly as possible into "real Americans." The subtle (and not so subtle) racism and the rearticulation of patterns of cultural domination were certainly not invisible either to the students and community members or to many of the teachers who strongly believed that these policies were immensely destructive both of the students' sense of self-worth and of the cultures and histories that needed to be cherished and nurtured, not destroyed.

For years, these and similar policies continued to be common practice. The story of the often-successful, concerted challenges to them is of immense importance. Yet, with the growth of the "English-only" movement and of the rightist assertion of the primacy of the (highly romanticized) "Western tradition" and other right-wing offensives, we are in danger of losing many of these gains. Cultural domination and the creation of the "other"—long facts of life in many of our institutions[1]—are coming center stage in the human drama of education as conservative triumphalism spreads out over the landscape.

For this reason, much of my argument in this book has depended on a particular position. Unreflective acceptance of neoconservative and neoliberal discourse as authoritative serves to enshrine certain interpretations of social and cultural life and to obscure others. This usually has the dual effect of advantaging dominant groups in society and disadvantaging subordinate ones.[2] Current proposals for national curricula, national testing, privatization and marketization, connecting schools more directly to an exploitative economy, and the accompanying growth of rightist sentiments will have these effects in quite predictable ways. Possessive individualism and authoritarian populism, rather than social justice, will be the result.

Neoliberals and neoconservatives, and especially the former, would argue that they are not unconcerned with social justice. The enhanced competition that will result from reorganizing society around the general principles derived from the market will produce improvements in the quality and number of services available to "consumers" who will have "freedom of choice." It is believed that this in turn will "enhance the wealth producing potential of the economy, thereby bringing about gains for the least well-off as well as for the socially advantaged." Thus, the market will actually lead to greater social justice for the least well off by placing choice in their hands.[3]

This series of claims is conceptually weak in terms of a justifiable theory of social justice, and even more weak empirically. As I argued in Chapter 2 and as recent research on such models inside and outside of education has shown, the results of such policies is likely to be an increasingly stratified society. Speaking about the growing neoliberal emphasis on privatization and marketization in education, Geoff Whitty provides a clear summary of a number of the dangers.

> The growing tendency to base more and more aspects of social affairs on the notion of consumer rights rather than citizen rights involves more than a move away from public-provided systems of state education towards individual schools competing for clients in the marketplace. While seeming to respond to critiques of impersonal over-bureaucratic welfare state provision, this also shifts major aspects of education decision-making out of the public into the private realm with potentially significant consequences for social justice. Atomized decision-making

within an already stratified society may appear to give everyone formally equal opportunities but will actually reduce the possibility of collective struggles that might help those least able to help themselves. As Henry Giroux and Peter McLaren put it, "Competition, mobility, getting access to information, dealing with bureaucracies, providing adequate health and food for one's children are not simply resources every family possesses in equal amounts." Because of this, the transfer of major aspects of educational decision-making from the public to the private realm undermines the scope of defending the interests of disadvantaged individuals and groups and thereby potentially intensifies these groups' disadvantage.[4]

Whitty concludes with a damning statement that the spread of such neoliberal economic models—when coupled with the focus of the neoconservatives on a strong state that regulates values, conduct, and the body—will *not* provide the context for active citizenship through which social justice can be pursued.[5] Instead, such reforms will provide ideal conditions for exacerbating existing inequalities.[6]

In this regard, R. W. Connell, one of our most perceptive authors on education, reminds us of some simple yet profound truths. He argues that there are three key reasons why all of us involved in schooling must be concerned with social justice. First, the entire educational system itself is a major public asset. As such, it is one of the "largest industries in any modern economy; it is one of the largest public undertakings." Yet, given the immense scale of this public asset, one of the most serious questions we should ask is, "Who gets most of its benefits?" This is a complex issue, but in terms of both access and outcomes, the educational system distributes social assets in ways that are more than a little unequal.[7]

Second, the educational system is likely to become more important as a public asset in the future,[8] in large part because organized knowledge has become increasingly crucial as a driving force within economic production, for the expansion and control of markets, and in establishing and maintaining the credential markets that support the social, sexual, and racial divisions of labor.[9] In Connell's words, "The educational system, then, not only distributes current social assets. It also shapes the kind of society that is coming into being. Whether our future society is a just one depends, in part, on the use we make of the education system now."[10]

Finally, Connell's third point concerns what it means to educate. For him, and for so many others, teaching is a "moral trade." When conservative Christian fundamentalists question the morality of education and the school's role in teaching particular kinds of morality, there is a very real moment of insight in their questions. Although I am in very strong disagreement with the authoritarian leanings underneath their partly populist position, portions of their intuitions seem eminently sensible to me. Along with Connell, we can turn these intuitions into a critique of the stratifying effects of current school practices. As social practices, "teaching and learning *always* involve questions about purposes and criteria for action (whether these purposes are shared or not), about the application of resources (including authority and knowledge), and about responsibility and the consequences of action." This very moral character of education directly affects the moral quality of the institutions that do the educating. If school systems consistently deal unjustly with many of their pupils, these pupils are not the only ones who suffer. *"The quality of education for all of the others is degraded."* [11]

In striking language, Connell concludes:

> I would like to shout this from the rooftops every time I hear another argument for "talented and gifted" programs, for tougher "standards" and stricter discipline, for streaming or tracking, for merit awards and opportunity schools and honors programs—in short, for any of the hundred and one affronts to equal provision of education. An education that privileges one child over another is giving the privileged child a corrupted education, even as it gives him or her a social or economic advantage. [12]

Connell's points are grounded in a social vision that demands that we pay attention both to our own rhetoric and to the hidden effects of many of our supposedly meritorious educational programs. I tend to be in strong agreement with what he says. Yet, something stops us from recognizing and acting on his arguments. Perhaps one of the reasons is the very way we think about schooling.

### MISREADING CONNECTIONS

In Arthur Conan Doyles's "The Naval Treaty," Sherlock Holmes and Dr. Watson report to the reader that

> Holmes was sunk in profound thought and hardly opened his mouth until we had passed Capham Junction.
> "It's a very cheery thing to come into London by any of these lines which run high and allow you to look down upon houses like this."

I thought he was joking, for the view was sordid enough, but soon he explained himself.

"Look at those big, isolated clumps of buildings arising above the slates, like brick islands in a lead-coloured sea."

"The board-schools."

"Light-houses, my boy! Beacons of the future! Capsules with hundreds of little seeds in each, out of which will spring the wiser, better England of the future."[13]


In this little vignette, we have nearly everything necessary to tell the story of schooling in this society as well as in Holmes and Watson's London. The school stands as a beacon of hope above the sordid conditions of poor and working class neighborhoods. It provides the seeds for individual mobility. Yet, these are *isolated* clumps of buildings, unconnected to the daily lives of that "lead-coloured sea." It is their very symbol as capsules above it all, that allows them to plant the seeds that will bring a "wiser, better" future. Holmes and Watson's conversation speaks to the tensions in our understanding of schooling. It embodies the hope that all of us have as educators—the hope of a better future for all children. Yet, at the same time, it appropriates an uncritical acceptance of the myth of schooling, the myth that schools—as "neutral institutions"—will provide an equal starting point for all who wish to run the race. Quite important, it also includes a subtext. It is a *class* story. The world is seen from above. The metaphors create a vision of rising up, of solid "brick islands" standing against a tide of dirty turbulence. A good school is one that is disconnected from the lives below, that ignores the sea. Popular culture and real lives are "sordid."

This vision is not limited to the world of fiction, nor is it held only by train riders like Watson and Holmes. Rather, many people, including many educators and neoconservative commentators, take a similar position. Anything "popular," anything from that sea, is "soiled." It is not quite serious knowledge. Because of this, too often we assume that popular literature, popular culture, popular mathematics and science are *failed* knowledge. It is not quite real. Popular knowledge is pathologized,[14] at least in comparison to the existing academic curriculum, which is seen as uplifting and neutral. Yet, the existing curriculum is never a neutral assemblage of knowledge. As I demonstrated in Chapters 2 and 3, it is always based on an assertion of cultural authority. The same must be said about schools. While there are many schools (and teachers) that are models of vitality and richness, the vast majority of schooling for the children of that "lead-coloured sea"—poor and working class students, girls and boys of color, and so many others—is not neutral: not in its means, and certainly not in its outcomes. Perhaps the best description is still that of Jonathan Kozol, who simply describes both the conditions and the results in words I quoted before—as "savage inequalities."[15]

Yes, that sea may seem sordid; but who controls the economic, social, and educational conditions that make it so? Whose vision of society, whose vision of what counts as real knowledge (and for whom) organizes the lives in classrooms in that sea?

Throughout this book, I have been at pains to demonstrate that these are among the most crucial questions to ask during a period of conservative restoration. The relationship between schooling and economic, political, and cultural power is not an afterthought. It is a constitutive part of the very being of schooling. Holmes and Watson's conversation speaks to this in hidden but no less powerful ways. Understanding this requires that we see schools—and the curricula, teaching, and evaluation that go on in them—in ways that do not make invisible these connections between what we do as educators and the larger relations of power.

In some fields of scholarship—the history of science comes to mind—a distinction is made between internalist and externalist analyses. In the former, we understand a phenomenon through the history of the development of the internal characteristics of a discipline itself. In the latter, we must see the connections between the development of a theory or an area and the larger social relations or the micropolitics of the research community that create the need or conditions for such developments.

While neoliberals and neoconservatives know better—they fully understand that schools are connected to larger economic, cultural, and ideological conflicts—in the field of education today most discussions of the content and organization of curricula and teaching have been strikingly internalistic. Or, when educators do turn to "external" sources, they travel but a short distance—to psychology. There seems to be a strong assumption that by coupling "better content" with new psychological theories, most of the issues of education will be solved. Yet, the dynamics that I have analyzed in the prior chapters of this book cannot be understood as problems of learning per se. They are *fundamentally* about competing social visions; they are *fundamentally* about different ways of naming the world. The political cannot be reduced to the psychological without living in a world divorced from the real stuff of schooling.

This problem speaks to the continuation of a very long history of borrowing our basic paradigms from a very limited range of disciplinary (and, in some postmodern positions, antidisciplinary) frameworks. The psychologization of educational theory and practice—although it has brought gains in a number of areas—unfortunately also has had a number of crucial limiting effects. It has, profoundly, evacuated critical cultural, political, and economic considerations from the purview of curriculum deliberations, except when these questions are forced on education by active social movements. As each of the chapters in this book demonstrates, it is nearly impossible to deal seriously with such things as curricula, testing, textbooks, students, and the whole array of daily events that are the warp and woof of educational policy and practice, in the absence of such considerations. In the process of creating the psychological individual, education has nearly lost any serious sense of the social structures and the race, gender, class, and religious relations that form these individuals in such powerful, and at times contradictory, ways. Furthermore, it is then unable to situate curricula, teaching, and assessment into their wider social context, a context that includes larger programs for democratic education and a more democratic society. Finally, because of all this, it leaves us with eviscerated visions of *critical* practice.[16] While perhaps not as uncritical as Holmes and Watson, overly psychologized discourse all too often does not include any systematic analysis of what Secada calls "the kinds of inquiry that will help us understand how opportunity is unequally distributed in this society, the role that . . . education plays in that stratification, and how we might reclaim the aegis of educational reform to include the creation of a fairer social order as a legitimate goal."[17]

It is for these very reasons that new, more critically oriented, "externalist" approaches are so important. For without a recognition of the socially situated character of *all* educational policy and practice, without a recognition of the winners and losers in this society, without a more structural understanding of how and why schools participate in creating these winners and losers,[18] I believe that we are doomed to reproduce an endless cycle of high or diminishing hopes, rhetorical reforms, and broken promises. This is why I have paid close attention to the complicated politics surrounding education and to the struggles both over "reforming" educational policy and practice and over how we think about these things.

## THE PRACTICAL AND THE CRITICAL

The very idea of "reform" is important here. For some people, including a much wider swath of the United States public than the rightist alliance, the role of "reform" is about raising the achievement scores on what academics have defined as high status knowledge. For others like myself, it entails a much more thoroughgoing reconstruction of the ends and means not only of education but of the relations of domination and subordination in the larger society. Thus, behind every story we tell about education—even if only tacitly—is a social theory about what this society "really is" and what it is necessary for educators and others to do to participate in either changing it or defending what already seems progressive. These theories or social visions may be in conflict.

We are in the midst of such conflicts today—and education sits at center stage. Of course, not every group has equal power to define the terms of these conflicts or to move resolutions of them toward its own agenda. In fact, as I have argued throughout this book, while there are multiple ideological forces at play in education and in all of our institutions, it is the conservative agenda that seems to be providing leadership in the discourse of education, and that unfortunately is providing the direction for a good deal of "reform" not only there but in other arenas concerning poverty, welfare, health care, and so much more.

In the early days of Margaret Thatcher's first government in Britain, she spelled out the evangelical aims of her political program. "Economics is the method," she said. But this was not all. "The aim is to change the soul."[19] And the soul was to be changed in a strikingly conservative direction. While Thatcher spoke for Britain, much the same could be said for what has happened and is continuing to happen in the United States.

I have critically discussed many of the attributes of the conservative restoration in earlier chapters and have no need to recapitulate all my arguments here. However, the aims and effects of this movement are all around us. Let me restate the four major tendencies for "changing the soul" of education.

1. Proposals for "choice" such as voucher plans and tax credits to make schools like the (thoroughly idealized) "free-market" economy, at the same time as budget cuts are forcing draconian measures on local school districts.
2. The movement in state legislatures and state departments of education, as well as at a national level, to mandate both teacher and student "competencies" and outcomes and to establish statewide and national curricula and testing, thereby

centralizing even more the control over teaching and curricula.

3. The increasingly effective assaults on the school curriculum—and teachers—for its supposedly anti-family and anti-free-enterprise bias, its "secular humanism," its lack of patriotism, and its neglect of "values" and the "Western tradition".

4. And the most powerful, the growing pressure to make only the needs of business and industry into the goals of the educational system. [20]

I do not believe that, taken together, these constitute a wise set of policies, although, as I also have tried to show, there are real elements of insight at work here that should not be dismissed out of hand. But, in my mind, any discussion of transformations in and defense of education must be evaluated on where it stands on this assemblage of issues. At the base of these issues is one question—Who benefits?—and it must be asked continually. Perhaps my fourth point about the needs of business and industry can provide a paradigm case here.

Let me take as an example something that is clearly present in a number of proposed "reforms" today. I refer to the call to develop curricula and strategies of teaching that are more closely connected to what Holmes and Watson saw no need for: the "lead-coloured sea" of daily life. This takes on even more importance since part of the conservative agenda is *itself* critical of schooling that limits itself to elite "academic" knowledge. Indeed, many spokespersons for groups who want a much closer linkage between education and the economy, especially neoliberals, are themselves more than a little adamant about having schools teach only those things that are directly connected to one's future practical role as a paid worker. Because of this, our analysis must be more subtle than simply decrying the neoconservative emphasis on a return to older visions of academic study. And although it may offer parts of an answer, the solution is not simply to call for the "practical" and for a curriculum that is more engaging to students, as do many of the people who stand behind the economic arguments examined in Chapter 4—as well as a number of the more child-centered advocates of integrated curricula who see themselves as opposed on pedagogic grounds to that economically oriented position.

Few people who have witnessed the levels of boredom and alienation among our students in schools will quarrel with the assertion that curricula should be more closely linked to "real life." This is not the issue. What really matters is the question of *whose* vision of real life counts. Take, for instance, a mathematics curriculum that places at its very center a goal of "mathematical literacy" for flexible job performance. The construction of "real life" here—preparation for paid work—usually is totally uncritical. It pushes to the margins any real concern with the actual and declining conditions under which so many people labor. It ignores what was demonstrated in Chapter 4: the steady movement toward low-wage, part-time, nonunionized, no-benefits, service sector employment for millions of American workers. Absent an integration of these kinds of issues directly into one's mathematics curricula, not only is the goal of using mathematics to prepare students for "real life" a partial fiction, but it institutionalizes as official knowledge only those perspectives that benefit those groups who already possess the most power in this society.[21]

Compare this with John Dewey's own appraisal of the dangers of defining education as a narrow practical activity supposedly designed to prepare one for the "world of work." Such an education, centered around a particular definition of the "practical," severed the connection between daily activity and critical understanding that was so necessary in any education worthy of its name. Thus, when Dewey argued for vocational education (redefined and for all people), he saw it as being constituted by "the full intellectual and social meaning of a vocation." Speaking in the language of his day, he insisted that this had to include "instruction in the historic background of present conditions; training in science to give intelligence and initiative in dealing with material and agencies of production; and study of economics, civics, and politics to bring the future worker into touch with the problems of the day and the various methods proposed for their improvement."[22] The "practical," then, could never be divorced from historical, ethical, and political understanding without losing something in the process. Schooling should never be seen as simply training for industries' needs.

This can be made clearer if we focus on the issue of the connection between training and the economy, a connection that is at the heart of much of the rhetoric over our supposedly declining economic productivity and lack of competitiveness. There are ways of thinking about this that do not largely ratify the neoliberal dream of reducing all education and training into simply one more adjunct to the industrial project.

In its proposed policies on education and training for workers, the Ontario Federation of Labour has articulated nine key positions, ones that seem to me to be essential as a set of beginning steps, and that provide a much more democratic alternative to the deadening realities that the students whose voices we heard in Chapter 4 experienced. It is worth quoting them at length here, since they take a very different position on what literacy—even in the most practical of all workplace skills and knowledge—is for and who it must actually benefit.

1. Training is a right. This right must be universal—available without barriers to all employed workers, displaced workers and people wanting to enter or re-enter the [paid] work force.

2. Training is a tool for greater equity. It is an instrument for overcoming the particular inequities in the labour market faced by women, visible minorities, native [people], the disabled, and immigrants.

3. Training is a fundamental part of the job. Employed workers must have access to training during working hours with full pay. Displaced workers and those entering the work force must have access to training with income support and necessary services such as child care and counselling.

4. Training rights include the opportunity, through paid educational leave, for workers to upgrade themselves to achieve a high school education.

5. The content of training must be geared to workers' needs as they see them and must be developmental. Skills should be taught in a way that goes beyond a particular job and leaves trainees better able to take on different tasks in the future. Training must increase workers' control over technology and their work.

6. Workers and their unions must have a central role in determining, at all levels, the direction of training.

7. Training for all workers should be funded by a new training tax on employers. The funds from this tax should be administered by a newly created . . . commission composed equally of labour and business representatives.

8. Training for displaced workers and people wishing to enter or re-enter the [paid] labour force should be funded out of general revenue. There should be [adequate] income support provided by an enriched . . . or new income support program. . . . Social services also must be provided.

9. Training programs should be carried out in conjunction with public education in situations in which labour has a much more significant voice. These institutions may have to modify their own structures and approaches, but they are an invaluable resource suited to channel-

ing training in a broader direction, sensitive to the needs of workers as clients, and accountable to the public.[23]

These are important statements. They both recognize the need for an education—here for adults—that is connected to that "lead-coloured sea" and also do not minimize the importance of practical "training" in this. But, we need to be very clear that this is not a substitute for a strategy for full employment, with jobs that have security, dignity, benefits such as health care, and decent pay. Nor can it be a substitute for programs that provide sufficient income support and a whole range of educational, health, housing, legal, and other services when people are forced to find alternative work.[24]

As with mathematical literacy, if training is to be effective, it first must not only meet the needs of the economy—needs that, like the issue of a common curriculum discussed in Chapter 2, must be defined by a much broader segment of the population than those who already possess economic, political, and cultural power. Second, the social category of employee is not sufficient to encompass the needs of *persons*.[25] Not only does such a category need to encompass what is entailed in the concept of person, but it must be based in what people already know and in the abilities they already have. It clearly requires as well the encouragement of critical questioning, discussion, and participation about its goals, content, and procedures. Finally, and of great importance, it should enable *persons* "to have more control of their jobs and work life," learn more about individual and collective rights,[26] and be connected to a larger, more participatory, social and educational vision than that of simply providing the "human capital" needed by business and industry. That it also should be part of a more extensive strategy of eliminating distinctions based on race, gender, class, and sexuality should go without saying.

So far I have talked about combining the "practical" with the "critical" and the "theoretical" in terms of adults. It is equally crucial to combine these with students in our elementary, middle, and secondary schools. This is especially the case for those students whose life on the margins is produced by the decisions of economically dominant groups, and then legitimated by the discourse of neoconservatives whose own vision of social justice seems to amount to no more than blaming the victim.

The danger residing within a totally practical emphasis for the children of the poor, dispossessed, and working class was recognized early on by the noted Italian political theorist and activist, Antonio Gramsci. He delivered a withering critique of schools that saw their job to be only satisfying "immediate, practical interests" under the guise of egalitarian rhetoric. Behind the democratic slogans, he warned, was a neglect of the overwhelming need to develop in students the capacity "to reason, to think abstractly while remaining able to plunge back from abstraction into real and immediate life, to see in each fact or datum what is general and what is particular, to distinguish the concept from the specific instance."[27] By limiting the school curriculum to only the practical problems of daily life, such schools left access to the skills of *critical* reasoning only to those who were already in dominance.[28] Think of the voices of the young people in the previous chapter who certainly had critical intuitions and nascent understandings of what this economy and their supposedly "practical" education meant for them. An education that did not connect with and expand on these critical intuitions would be disempowering.[29]

These points illuminate a very real tension in any educational program that seeks to take seriously the "lead-coloured sea" in more than rhetorical ways. On the one hand, it is important to take seriously the following question and answer: "How do you get someone to understand an abstraction? By relating it to the reality that it is an abstraction of."[30] On the other hand, the point of this entire discussion from Dewey to Gramsci is not simply to call for pedagogies that only and perhaps obliquely connect with student sensibilities. Indeed, we need to be extremely careful that such educational strategies are not pedagogies of *individual adaptation* rather than pedagogies of social transformation. Practical and "progressive" teaching and curricula are not always socially critical. In a highly stratified society such as the one in which we live, "experiential, affective and emotional learning can shape dispositions and loyalties" just as easily in directions favoring the powerful as the least advantaged. It can inhibit, not enhance, the development of dispositions of rigorous critique.[31] We, thus, need to ask of each and every proposed "reform" in schools whether its analysis and proposals are indeed linked to the development of such critical dispositions.

Students themselves are often quick to determine whether a focus on real life is serious or not. If it does not connect in powerful ways to their daily experiences, many students simply will return to the "cynical bargain" of doing just enough to get by that Linda McNeil has shown characterizes so much of their school experience.[32] This makes Gloria Ladson-Billings's recent accounts of how teachers critically connect their teaching to the realities of students' lives and material conditions even more important, since they clearly are guided by a critical appraisal of how all too much of the education offered to African American students and so many other children of color in this society has the effect of *disqualifying* a majority of these children, especially in times of severe economic and social dislocation. As Ladson-Billings shows, it is possible to combine socially just curricula and teaching with an emphasis on students' popular culture and at the same time not ignore the dominant knowledge that is the cultural capital of the powerful. Thus, by starting with a socially critical answer to the question, "Who benefits?" Ladson-Billings is able to tell the story of African American teachers who have taken Gramsci's points seriously in their daily actions and have reversed the process by which educational benefits are distributed.[33] We have much to learn from such stories, especially about how we might practically counter the neoconservatives' emphasis on tighter cultural control and more stratified schooling.

## BEING HONEST WITH OURSELVES

Everything I have said here requires that we place even our best efforts at educational "reform" back into the macro- and micro-relations of power inside schools, and between schools and the relations of exploitation and domination that provide the social context in which education operates. It assumes that whether our attempts at creating more responsive curricula and teaching succeed is dependent on a realistic and critical assessment of the conflicting forces at work inside schools and the larger society. I have claimed in this book that our aim should be not only the formation of "critical literacy" in our students but, in essence, becoming more critically literate ourselves about the economy, about cultural conflicts, and about the role of the state. As I argued, too much of the literature on reforming education evacuates such social questions. Even the literature that expressly deals with some aspects of how schools may fail an increasingly large population of students (e.g., the material on dropouts and "at risk" students) does this by once again tacitly psychologizing the problem.

Take the language of reforms to assist "at risk" students, a language that lies behind much of the discourse analyzed in Chapter 4. The social construction of what the "problem" is, diverts our attention from some of the most important root issues. Michelle Fine articulates the point in the following way:

To position students as "at risk" bears potentially two very distinct sets of consequences. The benevolent consequence is that their needs could in fact be attended to. The notion of "at risk" . . . also offers a deceptive image of an isolatable and identifiable group of students who, by virtue of some personal characteristic, are not likely to graduate. As Foucault would argue, the image betrays more than it reveals. Diverted away from an economy that is inhospitable to adolescents and adults, particularly U.S.-born African-Americans and Latinos, and diverted from the collapsing manufacturing sectors of the country, housing stock, and impoverished urban schools, our attention floats to the individual child, his/her family, and those small-scale interventions which would "fix" him/her as though their lives were fully separable from ours.

> [They] divert social attention to individual children and adolescents, their families, and communities. . . . [While they do] indeed represent "real" issues, more dangerously, however, at the same time they are imaginary. They reproduce existing ideologies, shave off alternative frames and recommend as "natural" those programs of reform which serve only to exacerbate class, race, and gender stratifications.[34]

Aside from the dangerous stereotyping that labels such as "at risk" reproduce and create, we tend to come up with simplistic "solutions" in our responses to "at risk" youth, plans that may be useful *as part of a larger strategy* of social and educational transformation but that as an isolated intervention falter on the shoals of the massive reality and depth of the problems education confronts. This can be seen, for instance, in the argument that greater involvement of parents is "the answer" to the problems of school achievement of "at risk" students in our urban areas.

After deep involvement in and research on reforms aimed at parental involvement—although much the same can be said of many reforms in general—Michelle Fine again puts it well.

> The assumption that empowered and involved parents produce educated students can be laid to rest. . . . Empowered parents . . . do not, in and of themselves, produce in the aggregate improved student outcomes in the areas of retention, absenteeism, California Achievement Test scores, or grades. Parental involvement is necessary but not sufficient to produce improved student outcomes. Without a serious national, state, and community commitment to serving children broadly, and to reconstructing schools in low income neighborhoods and their surrounds, deep parental involvement with schools will do little to positively affect—or sustain—low income students or their schools and outcomes.[35]

While Fine does not have in mind the argument in Chapter 3 about how important a more responsive school—that listens carefully to parents without stereotyping their concerns—can be in interrupting the growth of the Right at a local level, she does make a number of perceptive arguments. Thus, she seems to be more than a little correct when she argues that focusing on only one element—here, parental involvement in economically depressed and racially segregated areas—misses the depth of the problem and what may be necessary for lasting transformations. As she notes, over the past decade, federal and state governments have tried to shift the responsibility and blame for educational problems onto the backs of low-income parents. But, individual parental involvement projects cannot restore a rich, critical, and creative public sphere. Only with a powerful, supportive, and activist national agenda for children can parental involvement thrive, and then only if it provokes thoughtful, critical inquiry into public bureaucracy. [36]

These points have very real implications for more general educational reforms. Attempts at *partly* democratizing educational decision making are occurring at almost precisely the "wrong" historical moment. This is a moment of severe public sector retrenchment, not expansion. "School-based resources and decision making have been narrowed, not expanded." For instance, many school-based councils that have been formed to "empower" local teachers and parents feel "empowered only to determine who or what will be cut." [37] Thus, defending what is there (which as I noted earlier may be extremely important in some circumstances), often becomes more important than transforming curricula or expanding one's educational horizons.

In this kind of situation, we should not be romantic. These new "equity-based" forms of school governance and teaching and curriculum development will take an immense amount of time. And this will have to take place in institutions where the intellectual and emotional labor of teaching is already intensified and where resources are often hard to find, even to keep buildings open the minimum number of days a year. [38] When this is coupled with the emotional and economic demands faced by parents and community members in these same geographical areas, it gives one reason to be a bit less sanguine about such reforms.

Thus, for Fine, and I wholeheartedly agree, as we continue to strive for the best educational experiences for our children in every curriculum area, we need to couple this with "relentless attention to *systematic* power and critique." [39] Anything less actually may serve to hide the ways existing realities of power systematically disenfranchise the least advantaged members of our communities. Without combining these two projects, we may be left with the scenario I discussed in earlier chapters of this book: An understandable emphasis on doing something now may exacerbate already existing social and cultural inequalities and actually may put in place further stratifying devices while shifting all the blame to the poor and their children. In a time when we are once again listening to social Darwinist and genetic arguments about why the poor are poor and why they do poorly in schools,[40] this would be a profoundly dangerous move.

## ON NONREFORMIST REFORMS

Asking, as I have done here, about who will benefit from the hard work we are doing is a painful enterprise. All educators (one would hope) are deeply committed to making schools better places to be. Efforts to improve the curricula and teaching that go on in these institutions continue to be crucial. Linking them to larger democratic struggles, to social movements that aim to overcome gender, class, and race inequalities inside and outside the school, is now more important than ever. Most of us can point to immensely talented and hard working educators and community activists who daily give their lives to create more socially critical and responsive school experiences. Yet, what of the experiences of the millions of other children in that "lead-coloured sea" who face the savage inequalities that so deeply scar this nation, inequalities that speak volumes about the commitments of dominant groups to this society's children?

My comments in this chapter are not meant to imply that approaches that focus on new forms of pedagogy, curricula, assessment, or decision making are not worthy. This is an unusual period of ferment in education, and alongside the rightist assaults a good deal of progress is being made in building more thoughtful and socially and personally sensitive programs.[41]

I am not asking us to embrace a fatalism that holds that it is impossible to change schools unless the social and economic relations of the wider society are transformed first. After all, such a model of analysis forgets that schools are not separate from the wider society, but are *part* of it and participate fully in its logics and sociocultural dynamics. Struggling in the schools *is* struggling in society. Further, as public schools such as Fratney Street School in Milwaukee, Central Park East School in New York City, the Rindge School of Technical Arts in the Boston area, and schools elsewhere demonstrate daily, it is possible to create an education that highlights and opposes in practice social inequalities of many kinds, helps students to investigate how their world and their lives have come to be what they are, and seriously considers what might be done to bring about substantial alterations in all of this. [42] Creating such an education also requires no small alteration in the ways teaching and learning are organized, the connections between this and the community, and the objectives that guide what the school is about. These public schools can give us hope that such gains are indeed possible even in times of conservative triumphalism. However, as I claimed, for these changes to last and to grow, educators working in and with schools such as these need a much more searching and honest appraisal of society, of how it is now organized to *deny* the probability of large-scale success, and of what larger educational, social, and cultural movements they can join to alter this.

I take the attempts to build more just and caring models of curricula and teaching as crucial first steps, and I believe that they must be supported. But I want to take some of the "fun" out of doing it. This is not to fill the role of Michael Apple as "Grinch." After all, there should be some measure of joy in working with students, teachers, and community members in schools and jointly creating the conditions necessary for success. As someone who spent a number of years teaching in inner city schools, I would never remove that joy. But let us not be romantic. Let us not act as if the problems of any one curriculum area—whether mathematics, science, literacy, or any other—can be "solved" in isolation from those of other subject areas, by adding more material on "popular culture," or in isolation from the problems of the entire school system itself whose *overall* structure (not only in urban areas) is too often authoritarian and/or manipulative in its relationship to students, teachers, and community members. Let us not assume, as proposals for standardized national curricula and a national test do, that tighter control will effectively do other than place the blame on these same students, teachers, and parents. Let us not act as if our main task is getting a few more students to do well on the cultural capital of elite groups or simply making curricula more "practical." Let us not act in isolation from the larger social questions that give any serious concern for social justice its critical edge.

Much can still be accomplished. But what gives anyone the right to call something an "accomplishment" is that—unlike Dr. Watson and Mr. Holmes—they've come down from the train and entered the "lead-coloured sea." And they have found that what looks colorless

through the glasses of what Bourdieu called in Chapter 2 the "subli-
mated, refined, disinterested, and distinguished" riders of that train,
is instead a creative and moving river of democracy, of people wanting and struggling both for a better life for themselves and their
children and for a society that no longer denies the right to help
determine the course of that river. Holmes and Watson are fictions.
Educational justice, too, may remain a fiction unless we constantly
connect ourselves to these struggles for justice.

But, once again, I do not want to be misinterpreted here. I am not
arguing against local struggle—far from it, as the analysis in Chapter 3
demonstrates. Rather, I am making the point that these struggles
make sense only in terms of larger social concerns. The test of their
efficacy is their status as what, in *Education and Power*, I called *nonreformist reforms*. These are reforms that are attempts at both transforming the practices of schools as they exist now and defending democratic practices from, say, the rapaciousness of economic logics that
are rapidly expanding. However, they must have another characteristic. They are self-consciously linked to a larger social vision and to a
larger social movement. Yet, there are hundreds of things that deserve action in schools. One chooses from among them those that
have the highest probability of expanding the sphere of further action, of creating more space for mobilization and for building upon
the principles of caring and social justice. It is this combination of
practical activity in schooling and potential for long-term continued
transformation that gives nonreformist strategies their power.

This position recognizes some of the insights in the arguments of
poststructuralists who claim that while there can be no utopian end
to relations of power, this does not mean that things cannot be different or better.[43] It goes further than this, though. It makes more concrete the claim that "getting better" can be justified only in terms of
one's relationship to concrete social movements. This it seems to me
to be a considerably wiser stance than the often cynical detachment
or simple pragmatism that expunges the need for a broader politics
and that is found in some of the postmodern and poststructural positions in education.

## IT AIN'T ALL LOCAL

There is a danger in saying what I said in the previous section.
The problems of schools are so compelling and the urge to get in
there and deal with what is happening to our children so understand-

ably powerful (like so many of you, I feel it like an ache in the gut every day) that we sometimes lose the capacity or do not have the time to step back and ask critical questions of the organization of the society in which we live. Nonreformist reforms quickly may become excuses for simple "reformism," for working in local sites such as schools—for, say, more parental involvement, better curricula, and so on—without struggling equally hard to make the connections to larger transformative movements. Because of this, I want to return us to a sense of these widespread social dynamics that organize and disorganize this society. Let us return to the historical points I raised in my earlier discussion of the workhouse test and how dominant groups often have constructed how poverty and its causes and results should be thought about and dealt with. Take race and the social construction of dependency as a case in point.

As Cornel West reminds us, the enslavement of Africans—over 20% of the population of the nation at the time—"served as the linchpin of American democracy." Thus, it is not an overstatement to suggest that "the much-heralded stability and continuity of American democracy was predicated upon black oppression and degradation."[44] Slavery as a legally sanctioned act may be over, but the racial structuring of this country is worsening every day.[45]

For decades new patterns of segregation have been clear and growing, as European Americans have moved to the suburbs and abandoned the inner cities. One result of this is that urban areas, in essence, have become "reservations," with majority African American and Latino/Latina populations and declining or disintegrating tax bases. Local governments in these urban areas are less and less able to meet even the basic needs of their citizens. The nation as a whole, in concert with these trends, is steadily moving toward a politics centered around the suburban vote. The growth of suburbanization enables white middle class voters to "fulfill communitarian impulses by taxing themselves for direct services (e.g., schools, libraries, police), while both ignoring urban decay and remaining fiscally conservative about federal spending."[46] This is an ideal situation for suburbanites since it allows them to shield their tax dollars from going into programs that benefit the poor and racial minorities.[47] And as conditions in the inner cities (and rural areas) worsen significantly, the structural relations that concretely tie suburban benefits to urban disintegration—in a manner so reminiscent both of the story of cheap french fries for the affluent and the destroyed lives of the people on that verdant plain and of the history of stable democracy and economic progress being bought at the cost of black slavery and exploitation—lead us to blame the poor for being too "dependent." This is not a new phenomenon for the United States in any way. It is why we need to combine *both* structural and poststructural understandings in order to understand the roots of our current dilemmas.

Historically, the United States has been especially hospitable to the development of the belief that dependency is "a defect of individual character." Given the fact that this country lacked a strong legacy of feudalism and aristocracy, the widespread popular sense of reciprocal relations between lord and "man" was underdeveloped. The older preindustrial meanings of dependency as an *ordinary, majority condition* that were widespread in, say, Europe were very weak here, and pejorative meanings were much stronger. Thus, whereas in the colonial period dependency was seen largely as a voluntary condition (except for the slave), as in being an indentured servant, the American Revolution "so valorized independence that it stripped dependency of its voluntarism, emphasized its powerlessness and imbued it with stigma."[48]

In their investigation of the very idea of dependency and its social uses in the United States, Nancy Fraser and Linda Gordon suggest the following:

> The American love affair with independence was politically double-edged. On the one hand, it helped nurture powerful labor and women's movements. On the other hand, the absence of a hierarchical social tradition in which subordination was understood to be structured, not characterological, facilitated hostility to public support for the poor. Also influential was the very nature of the American state, weak and decentralized in comparison to European states throughout the nineteenth century. All told, the United States proved fertile soil for the moral/psychological discourse of dependency.[49]

In current conditions, there is now increasing stigmatization of any dependency. "All dependency is suspect, and independence is enjoined on everyone."[50] Yet, it is wage labor that is the identifacatory sign of independence. In essence, "the worker"—one who is "self-supporting"—becomes the universal subject. Any adult who is not perceived to be a worker carries an immense burden of self-justification. After all, we all "know" that this economy and this nation have removed the barriers to work for anyone who really wants it. Yet, this is not a neutral description of reality, as the discussion in Chapter 4 clearly shows. It smuggles in a considerable number of normative claims, not least in its assumption that "the worker" has access to a job paying a living wage and is also not a primary parent.[51]

There are two major results of this. The first is to increase the already strong negative connotations associated with dependency. The second is to increase even more its individualization. Both are ideally suited to an articulation of the connections between race and gender and dependency that have played such a strong role in constructing dominant discourses in the nation's history. As I noted, seeing dependency as a character trait was already beginning to be widespread in the early years of the nation. This sense is given more power now that the legal barriers (e.g., formal and legally recognized overt segregation) supposedly have been ended. With the changes in coverture (the legal status of women in marriage) and Jim Crow brought about by the successful struggles by women and African Americans, it now has become possible for some groups to argue that equality of opportunity really exists; that it is individual merit, nothing else, that determines outcomes.[52] Fraser and Gordon put it in the following way:

> The groundwork for that view was laid by industrial usage, which defined dependency so as to exclude capitalist relations of subordination. With capitalist economic dependency already abolished by definition, and with legal and political dependency now abolished by law, postindustrial society appears to some conservatives and liberals to have eliminated every social structural basis of dependency. Whatever dependency that remains, therefore, can be interpreted as the fault of individuals. That interpretation does not go uncontested, to be sure, but the burden of argument has shifted. Now those who deny that the fault lies in themselves must swim upstream against the prevailing semantic currents. Postindustrial dependency is increasingly individualized.[53]

All of this is clear in my analysis of the economy and the placing of the blame on dropouts and schools. In this scenario, the poor indeed did get poor "the old fashioned way"; they earned it. They are dependent and therefore are the Other, either by reason of their individual character traits or by reason of their collective genetic endowment, as in *The Bell Curve*.[54] Either way, as in the case of suburbia or cheap french fries, it's not "our" problem.

We now face a situation in which "economic dependency" has become a synonym for the immense *creation* of poverty by the economic apparatus of this society. And with the sense that something of a new "personality disorder" called moral/psychological dependency is now in the air, talk of dependency as a fully *social relation of subordination* has become all too rare.[55] In the process, power and domination become invisible.

Changing this requires a thoroughgoing reconstruction of our understanding of how this society operates. One of the keys here is at the level of our common sense. We need to stop thinking—as the Right does—of the poor as "others," and instead need to substitute a vision of "us." This change needs to be accompanied by a restriction of market models of human activity to their appropriate, and very limited, boundaries. We should reassert the significance of positive freedom based on human dignity, community, and the realization of democracy in all of our institutions.[56]

Taking account of the real nature of the economy we reviewed in Chapter 4, all of this requires the reconstruction of our discourse about poverty and welfare, a reconstruction that seeks to regain our sense of ethics and community. Echoing some of R. W. Connell's points, Michael Katz argues that such a reconstitution needs to be based on five general tenets.

1. Reawakening our sense of moral outrage at the deadly persistence of homelessness, hunger, absent or inadequate health care, and other forms of deprivation.
2. Defending and enlarging the principles of human dignity, community, and the realization of democracy in concrete events in our daily lives, rather than the increasing emphasis on social Darwinist policies in the public arena.
3. Reinventing ways of insisting on and talking about poor persons not as "them" but as *us*.
4. Restricting market models to very limited spheres so that social justice—not profit and loss—provides the dominant lens through which we examine social and educational policies.
5. Strategically connecting these progressive points to other widely shared American values such as liberty by showing how poverty undermines families (of many kinds), community, the economy, and so on.[57]

While each of these points requires the development of detailed policies and sources of revenue, among the other major requirements are creative resources (something in abundance among *all* parts of the American population) and political will. The *fundamental* questions, however, are about "the basis of community, the conditions of citizenship, and the achievement of human dignity." In even starker terms, these questions are simply and profoundly about our definition of America, just how much we are willing to do to realize this definition, and who shall be engaged at all levels in deciding this.[58]

The spread of a rightist common sense will no doubt make this difficult. Yet, as argued in Chapter 3, it is not naturally preordained that the populist sentiments shared by many people must be organized around conservative social movements. The urge to have power over one's life, to actually be listened to by the state, and to care deeply about one's cultural roots and traditions, can provide the basis for a less authoritarian and more socially just formation as well. Thus, studying the Right, as I have done here, may be more important than we may realize. The rightists have recognized how important it is to build social movements that connect the local with the global. They have been more than a little successful in reorganizing common sense by engaging in a truly widespread educational project in *all* spheres of society—in the economy, in politics, and in the media and cultural apparatus. There are lessons to be learned here. The Right has proven that long-term engagement in cultural politics can be effective. Those of us who decry the authoritarian tendencies in their message could do worse than to study the ways in which such messages seem to successfully connect with the hopes, fears, dreams, and despairs of many people.

I am not asking us to copy some aspects of the Right, in their cynical, well-financed, and often manipulative politics. Rather, I am saying that something important has gone on here, something that is, in essence, one of the largest "educational" projects we have seen this century. Transformations of common sense take time and organization and commitment; but they also must make connections with people's daily lives if they are to be widely successful. These are not inconsequential points, especially because they are grounded in a position that asks critical educational studies to stop "amusing itself to death" in its metatheoretical flights away from the realities that are being constructed all around us. Such highly abstract work can be important, but in my mind *only* when it is consciously connected to oppositional social movements and not simply to academic status and mobility, as all too much of it is now.

In *Cultural Politics and Education* I have tried to steer a difficult path. I have employed some decidedly "heavy-duty" theory at times, but I have struggled to connect it explicitly to the project of understanding the concrete transformations that currently are having an impact on educational policy and practice. In doing this, I have made interventions into a number of areas: about how we should rethink the terms of what a common curriculum and common culture actually mean; about taking populist intuitions about the bureaucratic state seriously; and about refocusing our attention from the "problem" of the dropout and the "at risk" student to the structural patterns of economic opportunities now being made available and to the actual experiences of the people who do the work of this society. In highlighting these issues and their educational/political implications, I have moved back and forth between the global and the local. Such movement is conscious since it rejects the all too common split between the two. I refuse to engage in the act of privileging one over the other. Both are necessary. Each alone is insufficient. Thus, when I suggest that it is possible, and necessary, to interrupt the growth of the ultra-right at a local level by also interrupting the "gaze" of the state, this decidedly does *not* mean that more organized actions at a national level against the conservative restoration and its arrogant politics are any less important.

In making my claims here, I have brought together three kinds of arguments: cultural, political, and economic. None of these is reducible to the others. All are necessary to gain a more complex understanding of the limits and possibilities of educational work and of cultural work in general.[59] As I mentioned in my prefatory remarks in this book, one of the tragedies of some of the relatively uncritical growth of postmodern theories in critical educational studies has been that all too many people have begun to associate any serious discussion of the economy with essentialism and reductionism. This is not a good idea. As we showed in Chapter 3, for example, an analysis of the politics of oppositional identity formation that fuels the growth of antischool and antigovernment reaction, needs also to take account of economic fears and the nature of the economic transformations so many people are justifiably concerned about. And as we demonstrated in Chapter 4, it is crucial to deconstruct the false economic "reality" that is being constructed by economically powerful groups in their attempts both to export the blame for the economic crisis onto the schools and to convince the public that schools are to be interpreted only in terms of their effects on the production of "human capital."

All of this is central to cultural politics. We need to be concerned not only with whose knowledge gets to be declared "official" and what identities are formed—central questions in the debates over the politics of culture—but also with what discursive resources circulate that enable people to understand the world and their places in it. Economic discourse, organized around conservative agendas, plays a large part as a primary cultural resource for people to "know their place" (in both senses of that phrase) in the world. Hence, it must be taken very seriously, not only as a discourse, but as a set of very real material practices that help some groups and immiserate millions of others not only in the United States but throughout the world.

I am painfully aware that much more could and needs to be said about the programmatic implications of all that I have laid out. Two "howevers" are in order here. The first "however" is that in a relatively slim book, brief discussions inevitably must substitute for more detailed presentations. The second "however" follows from this and makes me feel a bit less worried about this problem than I otherwise might have been. As I noted in the Preface, issues of practice are and should be so crucial to all of us who are deeply committed to creating more caring and just educational institutions, that I made a decision to devote an entire, separate book to them. That book, *Democratic Schools*, presents the stories of four very real public schools as they successfully struggle to build and defend a critical education that is worthy of its name. Each story—told in the words of the educational activists who are engaged in the daily realities of actually doing it— documents that it is possible *now* to engage in counterhegemonic work, to establish ways of being with students, teachers, administrators, community members, and others, that do not reproduce the norms and values of the conservative alliance,[60] and that provide a possible context for expanding these gains into other spheres. Yet these stories are made much more meaningful and powerful if they are placed within the arguments I have articulated in *Cultural Politics and Education*. Understanding the cultural, political, and economic context of such efforts can make all the difference in their success. Otherwise we continue the lamentable tendency in education of ignoring the conditions that may make it possible or impossible for such struggles to succeed and grow.

Unfortunately, there are too many educators at universities throughout this country who are basically "experts for hire," or who are supposedly critical of what is happening today but who sit in their offices scrivening away at needlessly abstract academic "arcania." (This is *not* to say that theoretical work is unimportant. It is crucial, but largely when it is organic to groups who both recognize and struggle to deal with widespread relations of domination and exploitation.) They have become the Watsons and the Holmeses of our day. They assure us that the train is traveling in a direction that is "emancipatory" (or reject such phrases outright as somehow too "modernist"), as they gaze out from the windows at what their limited glasses see as a "lead-coloured sea." The only soil on their hands is from the ribbon on the printer attached to their computer. Rhetorical connections with politics are thrown down from the windows of the train as it speeds on its way to postmodern central. Isn't it reassuring that Holmes and Watson are on the case? In this case, my answer is no. Postmodern and poststructural theories are not meant to be thrown down as skeptical food for thought by Mannheimian "unattached intellectuals" from the train above. If taken seriously, and if *reconnected* with a structural sense of the patterned nature of realities that are not "merely" social constructions but truly deadly, they offer promising political and analytic tools. If not reconnected and if cynically deconstructive only, then my advice is to get off the train at the next stop.

These arguments point to the role of what many individuals are now calling the "public intellectual." The Right has more than its share of people like this. Shouldn't we have a few as well? Edward Said, from whom I drew a number of my arguments at the very beginning of this book, is worth turning to again at the end in this regard.

So pervasive has the professionalization of intellectual life become that the sense of vocation, as Julian Benda described it for the intellectual, has been almost swallowed up. Policy-oriented intellectuals have internalized the norms of the state, which when it understandably calls them to the capital, in effect becomes their patron. The critical sense is often conveniently jettisoned. As for intellectuals whose charge includes values and principles—literary, philosophical, historical specialists—the American university, with its munificence, utopian sanctuary, and remarkable diversity, has defanged them. Jargons of an almost unimaginable rebarbativeness dominate their styles. Cults like post-modernism, discourse analysis, New Historicism, deconstructionism, neo-pragmatism transport them into the country of the blue; an astonishing sense of weightlessness with regard to the gravity of history and individual responsibility fritters away attention to public matters, and to public discourse. The result is a kind of floundering about that is most dispiriting to witness, even as the society as a whole drifts without direction or coherence. Racism, poverty, ecological ravages, disease, and an appallingly widespread ignorance: these are left to the media and the odd political candidate during an election campaign. [61]

Said may be perhaps a bit too condemnatory at times about some of the political implications of theoretical approaches that are closely connected to new social movements, and he may overstate the supposedly glorious diversity and working conditions at most universities, but his overall points deserve applause, I think. Too many of "our" efforts amount to well-paid fiddling while Rome burns. Too many of them are not about anything of public importance. Perhaps too many of us like our french fries a little too much. For, in the end, we are talking about the lives and futures of our children. We must always remember the close connection between schooling and those cheap french fries.

# *Notes*

## PREFACE

1. Edward Said, *Culture and Imperialism* (New York: Vintage Books, 1993), p. xxii.

2. Michael W. Apple, *Official Knowledge: Democratic Education in a Conservative Age* (New York: Routledge, 1993).

3. Michael W. Apple, *Ideology and Curriculum*, 2nd edition (New York: Routledge, 1990), Michael W. Apple, *Education and Power* (New York: Routledge, 1985), and Michael W. Apple, *Teachers and Texts: A Political Economy of Class and Gender Relations in Education* (New York: Routledge, 1988).

4. Raymond Williams, *The Year 2000* (New York: Pantheon, 1983), pp. 243–269.

5. Richard Herrnstein and Charles Murray, *The Bell Curve* (New York: Free Press, 1994).

6. See Michael W. Apple, "Cultural Capital and Official Knowledge," in Michael Berube and Cary Nelson, eds., *Higher Education Under Fire* (New York: Routledge, 1994), pp. 91–107. I say *approaches* here because it is too easy to stereotype postmodern and poststructural theories. That would be unfortunate, since the political differences, for example, among the various tendencies associated with both, are often substantial.

7. Geoff Whitty, Tony Edwards, and Sharon Gewirtz, *Specialisation and Choice in Urban Education* (New York: Routledge, 1993), pp. 168–169.

8. Ibid., pp. 173–174.

9. Ibid., pp. 180–181.

10. Leslie Roman and Michael W. Apple, "Is Naturalism a Move Beyond Positivism?" in Elliot Eisner and Alan Peshkin, eds., *Qualitative Inquiry in Education* (New York: Teachers College Press, 1990), pp. 38–73.

11. See Carmen Luke and Jenny Gore, eds., *Feminisms and Critical Pedagogy* (New York: Routledge, 1992), and Cameron McCarthy and Warren Crichlow, eds., *Race, Identity, and Representation in Education* (New York: Routledge, 1993).

12. Terry Eagleton, *Literary Theory* (Minneapolis: University of Minnesota Press, 1983), p. 208.

13. See Apple, *Education and Power*.

14. Jim McGuigan, *Cultural Populism* (New York: Routledge, 1992), p. 61.

15. See Paul Willis, with Simon Jones, Joyce Canaan, and Geoff Hurd, *Common Culture* (Boulder: Westview Press, 1990), Henry Giroux, "Doing Cultural Studies: Youth and the Challenge of Pedagogy," *Harvard Educational*

*Review* 64 (Fall 1994), pp. 278–308, and Julia Koza, "Rap Music," *The Review of Education/Pedagogy/Cultural Studies,* in press.

16. That one can deal with popular culture and school culture together in elegant ways is very nicely documented in Matthew Weinstein, "Robot World: A Study of Science, Reality, and the Struggle for Meaning." Unpublished doctoral dissertation, University of Wisconsin, Madison, 1995.

17. Ian Hunter, in fact, argues that critical educational researchers are so wedded to schools that their criticisms function as part of the mobility strategies of an intellectual elite. This is provocative, but essentializing in the extreme. See Ian Hunter, *Rethinking the School* (St. Leonards, Australia: Allen & Unwin, 1994). See also my response to his book in Michael W. Apple, "Review of Ian Hunter, *Rethinking the School,*" *Australian Journal of Education, 39* (1995), pp. 95–96.

18. Education Group II, eds., *Education Limited* (London: Unwin Hyman, 1991), p. 33.

19. Apple, *Official Knowledge.*

20. William Reese, *Power and the Promise of School Reform* (New York: Routledge, 1986).

21. See, for example, Martin Carnoy and Henry Levin, *Schooling and Work in the Democratic State* (Stanford: Stanford University Press, 1985), and Didacus Jules and Michael W. Apple, "The State and Educational Reform," in William Pink and George Noblit, eds., *The Futures of Sociology of Education* (Norwood, NJ: Ablex, 1995).

22. Apple, *Education and Power.*

23. Michael W. Apple and James A. Beane, eds., *Democratic Schools* (Washington, DC: Association for Supervision and Curriculum Development, 1995). By focusing on the stories of a number of ongoing socially and educationally committed public schools run by educators who directly link their curricula and teaching to a clear sense of the economic, political, and cultural relations of power in the world, *Democratic Schools* gives what we believe is compelling evidence that the journey of hope in education continues in real schools with real teachers, students, and community members. If after you finish *Cultural Politics and Education,* you find yourself asking something like, "Okay, Apple, now what? What concrete ideas do you have for practicing what you preach? What alternatives would you propose, and what would you keep, to take your critical analysis seriously at the level of practice?" I can reply only that my answers to these questions are provided considerably more fully in *Democratic Schools.*

## CHAPTER 1

1. See, for example, Nancy Fraser, *Unruly Practices* (Minneapolis: University of Minnesota Press, 1989), pp. 144–187, and Bruce Curtis, *True Government by Choice Men?* (Toronto: University of Toronto Press, 1992).

2. Michael W. Apple, *Official Knowledge: Democratic Education in a Conservative Age* (New York: Routledge, 1993).

3. Geoff Whitty, Tony Edwards, and Sharon Gewirtz, *Specialisation and Choice in Urban Education* (New York: Routledge, 1993), pp. 48–49.

4. For more on this alliance or coalition, see Apple, *Official Knowledge*. On the new middle class and its own ideological tendencies and tensions, see Basil Bernstein, *The Structuring of Pedagogic Discourse: Class, Codes and Control*, Volume 4 (New York: Routledge, 1990).

5. I have discussed how these connections are made in Apple, *Official Knowledge*.

6. Allen Hunter, "The Politics of Resentment and the Construction of Middle America." Unpublished paper, Department of Sociology, University of Wisconsin, Madison, 1987, p. 23.

7. Ibid., p. 30.

8. Whitty, Edwards, and Gewirtz, *Specialisation and Choice in Urban Education*, p. 11.

9. David Robertson, "The Meaning of Multiskilling," in Nancy Jackson, ed., *Training for What? Labour Perspectives on Skill Training* (Toronto: Our Schools/Our Selves Education Foundation, 1992), p. 36.

10. Ian Hunter, *Rethinking the School* (St. Leonards, Australia: Allen & Unwin, 1994), p. 134. I do not necessarily agree with a number of the arguments in Hunter's book, but in this case he is more than a little insightful.

11. Ibid.

12. Whitty, Edwards, and Gewirtz, *Specialisation and Choice in Urban Education*, pp. 6–7. This is by far the best empirical study of the genesis and effects of rightist reforms.

13. Ibid., p. 11.

14. Quoted in Ted Honderich, *Conservatism* (Boulder: Westview Press, 1990), p. 196.

15. Quoted in Ibid., p. 197.

16. Ibid., p. 199.

17. Jonathan Kozol, *Savage Inequalities* (New York: Crown, 1991), p. 62.

18. Honderich, *Conservatism*, p. 160.

19. Ibid., p. 105.

20. Kozol, *Savage Inequalities*, pp. 193–194.

21. Jane Lewis, "Back to the Future: A Comment on American New Right Ideas About Welfare and Citizenship in the 1980s," *Gender and History* 3 (Autumn 1991), p. 326.

22. Ibid., p. 329.

23. Ibid.

24. Ibid., p. 331.

25. Ibid., p. 332.

26. Ibid.

27. Ibid., pp. 332–333. For an impressive analysis of the history of this process, see Nancy Fraser and Linda Gordon, "A Genealogy of Dependency," *Signs* 19 (Winter 1994), pp. 309–336.

28. See Stephanie Coontz, *The Social Origins of Private Life* (New York: Verso, 1988), and Stephanie Coontz, *The Way We Never Were* (New York: Basic Books, 1992).

29. Madeleine Arnot, "Feminism, Education and the New Right." Unpublished paper presented at the American Educational Research Association, Chicago, 1991, p. 15.

30. Ibid., pp. 15–16.

31. Ibid., pp. 25–26.

32. Ibid.

33. See Peter Bocock, *Hegemony* (New York: Tavistock, 1986), and Raymond Williams, *Marxism and Literature* (New York: Oxford University Press, 1977).

34. See Jim McGuigan, *Cultural Populism* (New York: Routledge, 1992), p. 63.

35. See Apple, *Official Knowledge*, for a more extensive discussion of these tendencies.

36. Bocock, *Hegemony*, p. 94.

37. McGuigan, *Cultural Populism*, p. 25.

38. See Michael Omi and Howard Winant, *Racial Formation in the United States*, 2nd edition (New York: Routledge, 1994), and Cameron McCarthy and Warren Crichlow, eds., *Race, Identity, and Representation in Education* (New York: Routledge, 1993).

39. Edward Said, *Culture and Imperialism* (New York: Vintage Books, 1993), p. xxv.

40. Ibid.

41. Arthur M. Schlesinger, *The Disuniting of America* (New York: Whittle Communications, 1991).

42. Said, *Culture and Imperialism*, p. xxvi. Italics in original.

43. Sherene Razack, "What Is to Be Gained by Looking White People in the Eye? Culture, Race, and Gender in Cases of Sexual Violence," *Signs* 19 (Summer 1994), p. 905.

44. Whitty, Edwards, and Gewirtz, *Specialisation and Choice in Urban Education*, p. 179.

45. Kozol, *Savage Inequalities*.

46. Pierre Bourdieu quoted in Loic J. D. Wacquant, "Towards a Reflexive Sociology," *Sociological Theory* 7 (Spring 1989), p. 46.

47. For a very different and considerably more progressive way of thinking about the relationship between education and work, see Walter Feinberg, *Japan and the Pursuit of a New American Identity* (New York: Routledge, 1993).

48. Fraser and Gordon, "A Genealogy of Dependency," p. 310.

## CHAPTER 2

1. Michael W. Apple, *Ideology and Curriculum*, 2nd edition (New York: Routledge, 1990), and Michael W. Apple, *Official Knowledge: Democratic Education in a Conservative Age* (New York: Routledge, 1993).

2. Michael W. Apple, *Teachers and Texts: A Political Economy of Class and Gender Relations in Education* (New York: Routledge, 1988).

3. See Basil Bernstein, *Class, Codes and Control*, Volume 3 (New York: Routledge, 1977), and Michael W. Apple, "Social Crisis and Curriculum Accords," *Educational Theory* 38 (Spring, 1988), pp. 191–201.

4. Pierre Bourdieu, *Distinction* (Cambridge, MA: Harvard University Press, 1984), p. 7.

5. Ibid., pp. 5–6.

6. Ibid., p. 2.

7. Geoff Whitty, "Education, Economy and National Culture," in Robert Bocock and Kenneth Thompson, eds., *Social and Cultural Forms of Modernity* (Cambridge: Polity Press, 1992), p. 292.

8. See Apple, *Teachers and Texts*, and Michael W. Apple and Linda Christian-Smith, eds., *The Politics of the Textbook* (New York: Routledge, 1990).

9. Ibid.

10. See Chapter 4 in this book. See also Sheldon H. Danziger and Daniel Weinberg, eds., *Fighting Poverty: What Works and What Doesn't* (Cambridge, MA: Harvard University Press, 1986), and Gary Burtless, ed., *A Future of Lousy Jobs?* (Washington, DC: The Brookings Institution, 1990).

11. See, for example, Stephen Jay Gould, *The Mismeasure of Man* (New York: W. W. Norton, 1981). Feminist criticisms of science are essential to this task. See, for example, Donna Haraway, *Primate Visions* (New York: Routledge, 1989), Sandra Harding and Jean F. Barr, eds., *Sex and Scientific Inquiry* (Chicago: University of Chicago Press, 1987), Nancy Tuana, ed., *Feminism and Science* (Bloomington: Indiana University Press, 1989), and Sandra Harding, *Whose Science, Whose Knowledge?* (Ithaca, NY: Cornell University Press, 1991).

12. Marshall S. Smith, Jennifer O'Day, and David K. Cohen, "National Curriculum, American Style: What Might It Look Like?" *American Educator* 14 (Winter 1990), pp. 10–17, 40–47.

13. Ibid., p. 46.

14. Ibid.

15. Ibid.

16. Ibid.

17. Ted Honderich, *Conservatism* (Boulder: Westview Press, 1990), p. 1.

18. Ibid., p. 4.

19. Ibid., p. 15.

20. See Apple, *Official Knowledge*.

21. I put the word "minority" in quotes here to remind us that the vast majority of the world's population is composed of persons of color. It would be wholly salutary for our ideas about culture and education to remember this fact.

22. Apple, *Official Knowledge*.

23. Apple, *Teachers and Texts*, and Apple, *Official Knowledge*.

24. Ann Bastian, Norm Fruchter, Marilyn Gittell, Colin Greer, and

Kenneth Haskins, *Choosing Equality* (Philadelphia: Temple University Press, 1986).

25. See Michael W. Apple, *Education and Power* (New York: Routledge, 1985).

26. Andy Green, "The Peculiarities of English Education," in Education Group II, eds., *Education Limited* (London: Unwin Hyman, 1991), p. 27.

27. Allen Hunter, *Children in the Service of Conservatism* (Madison: University of Wisconsin, Madison Law School, Institute for Legal Studies, 1988). Neoliberalism actually doesn't ignore the idea of a strong state, but it wants to limit it to specific areas (e.g., defense of markets).

28. Richard Johnson, "A New Road to Serfdom?" in Education Group II, eds., *Education Limited*, p. 40.

29. Quoted in Tony Edwards, Sharon Gewirtz, and Geoff Whitty, "Whose Choice of Schools?" in Madeleine Arnot and Len Barton, eds., *Voicing Concerns: Sociological Perspectives on Contemporary Educational Reforms* (London: Triangle Books, 1992), p. 156.

30. Ibid. The authors are quoting from Roger Dale, "The Thatcherite Project in Education," *Critical Social Policy* 9 (no. 3, 1989).

31. "Introduction to Part Three—Alternatives: Public Education and a New Professionalism," in Education Group II, eds., *Education Limited*, p. 268.

32. Johnson, "A New Road to Serfdom?" p. 68.

33. Honderich, *Conservatism*, p. 104.

34. Ibid., pp. 99–100.

35. Ibid., p. 89.

36. Ibid., p. 81.

37. Whitty, "Education, Economy and National Culture," p. 294.

38. Ibid.

39. Green, "The Peculiarities of English Education," p. 29.

40. Ibid. I am making a "functional" not necessarily an "intentional" explanation here. See Daniel Liston, *Capitalist Schools* (New York: Routledge, 1988). For an interesting discussion of how such testing programs may actually work against more democratic efforts at school reform, see Linda Darling-Hammond, "Bush's Testing Plan Undercuts School Reforms," *Rethinking Schools* 6 (March/April, 1992), p. 18.

41. Johnson, "A New Road to Serfdom?" p. 79. Italics in original.

42. Ibid., pp. 79–80.

43. Ibid., p. 80. See also Elizabeth Ellsworth, "Why Doesn't This Feel Empowering?" *Harvard Educational Review* 59 (August 1989), pp. 297–324.

44. See Steven Best and Douglas Kellner, *Postmodern Theory: Critical Interrogations* (London: Macmillan, 1991), pp. 34–75.

45. Richard Johnson, "Ten Theses on a Monday Morning," in Education Group II, eds., *Education Limited*, p. 320.

46. See Apple and Christian-Smith, eds., *The Politics of the Textbook*, Apple, *Official Knowledge*, and Whitty, "Education, Economy and National Culture," p. 290.

47. Johnson, "Ten Theses on a Monday Morning," p. 319. See E. D. Hirsch, Jr., *Cultural Literacy* (New York: Houghton Mifflin, 1986).

48. Johnson, "A New Road to Serfdom?" p. 51. See also Susan Rose, *Keeping Them out of the Hands of Satan* (New York: Routledge, 1988).

49. "Preface," Education Group II, eds., *Education Limited*, p. x. Speaking of Britain (but much the same can be said about the United States), Homi Bhabha puts the international sense well. "The Western metropole must confront its postcolonial history, told by its influx of postwar migrants and refugees, as an indigenous or native narrative *internal to its national identity*; and the reason for this is made clear in the stammering, drunken words of Mr. 'Whiskey' Sisodia from *The Satanic Verses*: 'The trouble with the Engenglish is that their hiss history happened overseas, so they dodo don't know what it means.'" (Italics in original.) See Homi K. Bhabha, *The Location of Culture* (New York: Routledge, 1994), p. 6.

50. Johnson, "A New Road to Serfdom?" p. 71.

51. Ibid.

52. For a more complete analysis of racial subtexts in our policies and practices, see Michael Omi and Howard Winant, *Racial Formation in the United States*, 2nd edition (New York: Routledge, 1994), and Cameron McCarthy and Warren Crichlow, eds., *Race, Identity, and Representation in Education* (New York: Routledge, 1993).

53. Johnson, "A New Road to Serfdom?" p. 82.

54. See Apple, *Official Knowledge*.

55. See the compelling accounts in Jonathan Kozol, *Savage Inequalities* (New York: Crown, 1991).

56. Basil Bernstein, *The Structuring of Pedagogic Discourse: Class, Codes and Control*, Volume 4 (New York: Routledge, 1990), p. 63.

57. Ibid., p. 64.

58. Ibid., p. 87.

59. Ibid.

60. Geoff Whitty, "Recent Education Reform: Is It a Post-Modern Phenomenon?" Unpublished paper presented at the Conference on Reproduction, Social Inequality, and Resistance, University of Bielefeld, Bielefeld, Germany, October 1–4, 1991, pp. 20–21.

61. Compare this with the United States experience in Michael W. Apple and Susan Jungck, "You Don't Have to Be a Teacher to Teach This Unit," *American Educational Research Journal* 27 (Summer 1990), pp. 227–251.

62. Edwards, Gewirtz, and Whitty, "Whose Choice of Schools?" p. 157.

63. Green, "The Peculiarities of English Education," p. 30. For further discussion of the ideological, social, and economic effects of such "choice" plans, see Stan Karp, "Massachusetts 'Choice' Plan Undercuts Poor Districts," *Rethinking Schools* 6 (March/April 1992), p. 4, and Robert Lowe, "The Illusion of 'Choice,'" *Rethinking Schools* 6 (March/April, 1992), pp. 1, 21–23.

64. Geoff Whitty, personal correspondence. Andy Green, in the English context, argues as well that there are merits in having a *broadly defined* na-

tional curriculum, but goes on to say that this makes it even more essential that individual schools have a serious degree of control over its implementation, "not least so that it provides a check against the use of education by the state as a means of promoting a particular ideology." See Green, "The Peculiarities of English Education," p. 22. The fact that a large portion of the teachers in England, in essence, went on strike—actively refused to give the national test—provides some support for Whitty's arguments.

65. See Apple and Christian-Smith, *The Politics of the Textbook.*

66. Apple, *Ideology and Curriculum*, pp. xiii–xiv.

67. Raymond Williams, *Resources of Hope* (New York: Verso, 1989), pp. 35–36.

68. Ibid., pp. 37–38.

69. Ibid., p. 38.

70. See Apple, *Official Knowledge.*

71. Whitty, "Education, Economy and National Culture," p. 22.

72. See the discussion in Kozol, *Savage Inequalities.*

## CHAPTER 3

1. Joan Delfattore, *What Johnny Shouldn't Read* (New Haven: Yale University Press, 1992).

2. See Michael W. Apple, *Official Knowledge: Democratic Education in a Conservative Age* (New York: Routledge, 1993), Michael B. Katz, *The Undeserving Poor* (New York: Pantheon, 1989), and Jonathan Kozol, *Savage Inequalities* (New York: Crown, 1991).

3. See Bruce Curtis, *True Government by Choice Men?* (Toronto: University of Toronto Press, 1992) for an insightful example of the integration of these often disparate programs of analysis.

4. Michael W. Apple, *Teachers and Texts: A Political Economy of Class and Gender Relations in Education* (New York: Routledge, 1988), and Apple, *Official Knowledge.*

5. Geoff Whitty, Tony Edwards, and Sharon Gewirtz, *Specialisation and Choice in Urban Education* (New York: Routledge, 1993).

6. Apple, *Official Knowledge.*

7. These assumptions may not be exactly the same in other nations, especially regarding the relative power of religious fundamentalism. Further, not all segments of the cultural and religious right agree. For ease of presentation here, however, we will gloss over some of the differences within this movement.

8. Allen Hunter, *Children in the Service of Conservatism* (Madison: University of Wisconsin, Madison Law School, Institute for Legal Studies, 1988), p. 63.

9. Ibid.

10. Ibid., p. 15.

11. Ibid. It is important not to see such positions as "irrational." For many right-wing women, for example, such a belief is wholly sensible given the conditions in which they live. Joan Sherron DeHart gets it exactly right when she states that "we must recognize the screams of antifeminist women as the rational responses of people who live in a deeply gendered and profoundly precarious world—a world in which identity, social legitimacy, economic viability and moral order are deeply rooted in conventional gender categories." See Joan Sherron DeHart, "Gender on the Right: Behind the Existential Scream," *Gender and History* 3 (Winter 1991), p. 261.

12. Apple, *Official Knowledge*.

13. Tim La Haye, quoted in Hunter, *Children in the Service of Conservatism*, p. 57.

14. Hunter, *Children in the Service of Conservatism*, p. 57.

15. See Michael W. Apple and Linda Christian-Smith, eds., *The Politics of the Textbook* (New York: Routledge, 1991).

16. Delfattore, *What Johnny Shouldn't Read*, p. 123.

17. See Apple, *Teachers and Texts*, Apple, *Official Knowledge*, and Apple and Christian-Smith, eds., *The Politics of the Textbook*.

18. Delfattore, *What Johnny Shouldn't Read*, p. 139.

19. Rebecca Klatch, *Women of the New Right* (Philadelphia: Temple University Press, 1987), p. 23.

20. Ibid., p. 24.

21. Ibid.

22. Ibid., p. 26.

23. George Gilder, quoted in Klatch, *Women of the New Right*, pp. 28–29.

24. Klatch, *Women of the New Right*, p. 29.

25. Nancy Fraser, *Unruly Practices* (Minneapolis: University of Minnesota Press, 1989).

26. See Delfattore, *What Johnny Shouldn't Read*.

27. See Apple, *Official Knowledge*, and Apple and Christian-Smith, eds., *The Politics of the Textbook*.

28. Curtis, *True Government by Choice Men?*, p. 9, Curtis's emphasis.

29. Ibid., p. 5, our emphasis.

30. Ibid., p. 32. Curtis adds domination and exploitation to this list.

31. Ibid., p. 172.

32. Ibid., p. 175.

33. Ibid., p. 174.

34. Ibid., p. 192. See also Apple, *Official Knowledge*, pp. 64–92.

35. Curtis, *True Government by Choice Men?*, p. 197.

36. The material in this section is drawn from Anita Oliver, "The Politics of Textbook Controversy: Parents Challenge the Implementation of a Reading Series." Unpublished doctoral thesis, University of Wisconsin, Madison, 1993.

37. We want to be cautious not to overstate our reading of the class dynamics of this situation. The new middle class is itself divided. Not all fractions of it support "invisible pedagogies" such as whole language ap-

proaches. Basil Bernstein hypothesizes that those members of the new middle class who work for the state are much more likely to support such loosely classified and loosely framed pedagogies than those who work in the private sector. This, and particular professional ideologies, may account in part for the fact that most teachers, though not all, in Citrus Valley supported the whole language emphasis found in the state guidelines and in *Impressions*.

38. See Apple, *Teachers and Texts*, especially pp. 81–105.

39. About the same time that parents first complained about the books, some teachers also brought complaints, but of a very different nature. Teachers reported that some of the stories in the books did not match the table of contents in the student anthologies. Obviously, there was a distinct possibility that the wrong books had been shipped or that there were misprints. However, as the conflict intensified, the local teachers' union became increasingly vocal in its support for the *Impressions* series and for the school district administration. Of all the groups involved in this study, teachers were the most reluctant to be interviewed. This is understandable given the tensions and fear in this situation.

40. Fraser, *Unruly Practices*, pp. 113–144. See also Michael W. Apple, "Texts and Contexts: The State and Gender in Educational Policy," *Curriculum Inquiry*, 24 (Fall 1994), pp. 349–359.

41. See Francis A. Schaeffer, *The Francis A. Schaeffer Trilogy* (Westchester, IL: Crossway Books, 1990).

42. See, for example, Philip Wexler, *Becoming Somebody* (New York: Falmer Press, 1992).

43. How the state itself is transformed in this process is, of course, worthy of inquiry in this regard, but that will have to wait until another investigation.

44. See, for example, the widely discussed and hopelessly flawed volume by Richard Herrnstein and Charles Murray, *The Bell Curve* (New York: Free Press, 1994). The sponsorship of this volume and its authors by conservative foundations, and these groups' ability to place the authors on highly visible media outlets, is worth noting. It would be important to investigate the role of such conservative groups in sponsoring and circulating, and thus helping to make publicly legitimate, positions that have been discredited scientifically many times before.

45. See Apple, *Official Knowledge*, pp. 61–62.

46. Examples of more democratic responses can be found in Michael W. Apple and James A. Beane, eds., *Democratic Schools* (Washington, DC: Association for Supervision and Curriculum Development, 1995).

47. Ibid.

## CHAPTER 4

1. Marian Wright Edelman, "Introduction," in Arloc Sherman, *Wasting America's Future: The Children's Defense Fund Report on the Costs of Child Poverty*

(Boston: Beacon Press, 1994), p. xxiii. The term "at risk" itself is decidedly problematic, since it basically places the blame on the characteristics of the child rather than on the socially produced conditions in which she or he lives. It also implies some very dangerous stereotypes that can lead to a self-fulfilling prophesy.

2. Martin Carnoy, Derek Shearer, and Russell Rumberger, *A New Social Contract* (New York: Harper & Row, 1983), p. 61.

3. For further discussion of this, see Michael W. Apple, *Teachers and Texts: A Political Economy of Class and Gender Relations in Education* (New York: Routledge, 1988), and Michael W. Apple, *Education and Power*, 2nd edition (New York: Routledge, 1995).

4. Apple, *Teachers and Texts*. Apple has written extensively on the importance of a "relational" and nonreductive approach to the connections between education and the larger society and has warned us not to be overly economistic in our analyses. However, it is important to be reminded that even with these arguments, economic dynamics are among the most powerful forces in capitalism. For further discussion of this nonreductive program, see Apple, *Education and Power*.

5. The original data were initially reported in Apple, *Teachers and Texts*. This chapter goes significantly beyond these initial data, in both scope and currency of findings.

6. U.S. Bureau of the Census, *Money Income of Households, Families, and Persons in the United States: 1992* (Washington, DC: U.S. Government Printing Office, Current Population Reports, Series P60–184, 1993), p. xviii.

7. Ibid., pp. B-13, B-14.

8. Carnoy, Shearer, and Rumberger, *A New Social Contract*, pp. 22–23.

9. George Thomas Kurian, *The New Book of World Rankings* (New York: Facts on File, 1991), p. 73.

10. Ibid., p. 72.

11. International Bank for Reconstruction and Development/The World Bank, *Social Indicators of Development: 1994* (Baltimore, MD: Johns Hopkins University Press, 1994).

12. Sherman, *Wasting America's Future*, p. 81.

13. Ibid.

14. U.S. Bureau of the Census, *Poverty in the United States: 1992* (Washington, DC: U.S. Government Printing Office, Current Population Reports, Series P60–185, 1993), p. viii.

15. Sherman, *Wasting America's Future*, p. 4.

16. Wright Edelman, "Introduction," p. xvi.

17. U.S. Bureau of the Census, *Poverty in United States*, p. xi.

18. Ibid., p. viii.

19. Joshua Cohen and Joel Rogers, *On Democracy: Toward a Transformation of American Society* (New York: Penguin Books, 1983), p. 31. The official poverty income level and rate fluctuate, of course, and are manipulated for political purposes.

20. Wright Edelman, "Introduction," p. xxi.

21. Ibid., p. xxiii.

22. Ibid., p. xix.

23. Ibid.

24. Ibid., p. xvii.

25. Sherman, *Wasting America's Future*, p. 18.

26. Ibid., p. 62.

27. Ibid.

28. Wright Edelman, "Introduction," p. xx.

29. Ibid.

30. David T. Ellwood and Lawrence H. Summers, "Poverty in America," in Sheldon H. Danziger and Daniel Weinberg, eds., *Fighting Poverty: What Works and What Doesn't* (Cambridge, MA: Harvard University Press, 1986), p. 82.

31. U.S. Bureau of the Census, *Measuring the Effects of Benefits and Taxes on Income and Poverty: 1992* (Washington, DC: U.S. Government Printing Office, Current Population Reports, Series P60–186RD, 1993), p. 24.

32. Ibid., pp. 28, 30.

33. Ibid., p. 24.

34. Sheldon H. Danziger, Robert H. Haveman, and Robert D. Plotnick, "Antipoverty Policy: Effects on the Poor and the Nonpoor," in Danziger and Weinberg, eds., *Fighting Poverty*, p. 69.

35. Ellwood and Summers, "Poverty in America," p. 81.

36. U.S. Bureau of the Census, *Measuring the Effects of Benefits and Taxes on Income and Poverty: 1992*, p. xix.

37. Michael W. Apple, *Official Knowledge: Democratic Education in a Conservative Age* (New York: Routledge, 1993).

38. Gary Burtless, "Public Spending for the Poor: Trends, Prospects, and Economic Limits," in Danziger and Weinberg, eds., *Fighting Poverty*, p. 48.

39. U.S. Bureau of the Census, *Money Income of Households, Families, and Persons in the United States: 1992*, pp. x–xi.

40. Ibid., pp. 92–93.

41. Ibid., p. xii. The median yearly income of black female householders was $13,159; for Hispanic female householders, $13,289.

42. Sherman, *Wasting America's Future*, p. 3. The 1992 poverty line income for families of four was $14,335.

43. U.S. Bureau of the Census, *Statistical Abstract of the United States: 1994* (Washington, DC: U.S. Government Printing Office, 1994), p. 48.

44. Sherman, *Wasting America's Future*, p. 4.

45. U.S. Bureau of the Census, *Money Income of Household, Families, and Persons in the United States: 1992*, pp. 116, 130.

46. Ibid., p. xvi.

47. U.S. Bureau of the Census, *Measuring the Effects of Benefits and Taxes on Income and Poverty: 1992*, p. xxi.

48. U.S. Bureau of the Census, *Poverty in the United States: 1992*, p. 10.

49. U.S. Bureau of the Census, *Measuring the Effects of Benefits and Taxes on Income and Poverty: 1992*, p. 28.

50. U.S. Bureau of the Census, *Statistical Abstract of the United States: 1994*, p. 158.

51. U.S. Bureau of the Census, *Workers With Low Earnings: 1964–1990* (Washington, DC: U.S. Government Printing Office, Current Population Reports, Series P60-178, 1992), pp. 19–20.

52. U.S. Bureau of the Census, *Statistical Abstract of the United States: 1994*, p. 416.

53. Ibid.

54. *Economic Report of the President* (Washington, DC: U.S. Government Printing Office, 1994), p. 312.

55. William Julius Wilson and Kathryn M. Neckerman, "Poverty and Family Structure," in Danziger and Weinberg, eds., *Fighting Poverty*, p. 252.

56. *Economic Report of the President*, p. 312.

57. U.S. Bureau of the Census, *Statistical Abstract of the United States: 1994*, p. 88.

58. Ibid., p. 89.

59. Ibid., p. 100.

60. Ibid.

61. Ibid., p. 103.

62. Ibid., p. 13.

63. Jessie Carnie Smith and Robert L. Johns, eds., *Statistical Record of Black America* (Detroit: Gale Research Incorporated, 1995), pp. 104–105.

64. Ibid., p. 119.

65. Kathleen Maguire, Ann L. Pastore, and Timothy J. Flanagan, eds., *Sourcebook of Criminal Justice Statistics: 1992* (Washington, DC: U.S. Government Printing Office, U.S. Department of Justice, Bureau of Justice Statistics, 1993), p. 635.

66. Ibid., p. 576.

67. Ibid., p. 613.

68. U.S. Bureau of the Census, *Statistical Abstract of the United States: 1994*, p. 96.

69. Ibid., p. 66.

70. U.S. Bureau of the Census, *Statistical Abstract of the United States: 1994*, p. 80.

71. Ellwood and Summers, "Poverty in America," p. 99.

72. Charles V. Hamilton and Dona C. Hamilton, "Social Policies, Civil Rights, and Poverty," in Danziger and Weinberg, eds., *Fighting Poverty*, p. 307.

73. See the discussion of cheap french fries in Chapter 1.

74. U.S. Bureau of the Census, *Statistical Abstract of the United States: 1994*, p. 412.

75. Ibid., p. 429.

76. United Nations, *Statistical Yearbook* (New York: United Nations Department for Economic and Social Information and Policy Analysis, 1994).

77. Francis Green and Bob Sutcliffe, *The Profit System: The Economics of Capitalism* (New York: Penguin Books, 1987), p. 321.

78. U.S. Bureau of the Census, *Statistical Abstract of the United States: 1994*, p. 416.

79. Ibid., p. 173.

80. Green and Sutcliffe, *The Profit System*, pp. 321–322.

81. Paul Willis makes the provocative claim that one of the major consequences of high rates of youth unemployment will be on the ideological level. Since so many young men and women will not have pay checks, yet will still "hang out" in malls and shopping centers, they will consume products only with their eyes. This may subvert the basis of capitalism's wage accord with young laborers. The connection between consumption and paid work will be severed. The effect on patriarchal relations within working class households also can be immense. See Paul Willis, "Youth Unemployment: Thinking the Unthinkable." Unpublished paper, Wolverhampton Polytechnic, Wolverhampton, England, n.d.

82. Rebecca M. Blank and Alan S. Blinder, "Macroeconomics, Income Distribution, and Poverty," in Danziger and Weinberg, eds., *Fighting Poverty*, p. 191.

83. U.S. Bureau of the Census, *Statistical Abstract of the United States: 1994*, p. 412, Kathleen Droste, ed., *Gale Book of Averages* (Detroit: Gale Research Incorporated, 1994), p. 387, and Linda Schmittroth, ed., *Statistical Record of Women Worldwide* (Detroit: Gale Research Incorporated, 1994), p. 323.

84. Schmittroth, ed., *Statistical Record of Women Worldwide*, p. 387.

85. U.S. Bureau of the Census, *Workers With Low Earnings: 1964–1990*, p. 2.

86. U.S. Bureau of the Census, *Statistical Abstract of the United States: 1994*, p. 416.

87. Smith and Johns, eds., *Statistical Record of Black America*, p. 725.

88. Ronald Kutscher, "The Impact of Technology on Employment in the United States," in Gerald Burke and Russell Rumberger, eds., *The Future Impact of Technology on Work and Education* (Philadelphia: Falmer Press, 1987), p. 57.

89. Ibid. We have remained at the statistical level here, but it is important to keep reminding ourselves of the enormous social and emotional costs of being unemployed. No set of statistics can ever fully encompass the reality of these costs and of the lost lives they signify.

90. Donald N. McCloskey, *The Rhetoric of Economics* (Madison: University of Wisconsin Press, 1985), p. xix.

91. U.S. Department of Labor, Bureau of Labor Statistics, *Outlook: 1990–2005* (Washington, DC: U.S. Government Printing Office, 1992), p. 44.

92. Ibid.

93. Ibid., p. 43.

94. U.S. Bureau of the Census, *Statistical Abstract of the United States: 1994*, p. 410.

95. Kutscher, "The Impact of Technology on Employment in the United States," p. 46. Many of these emerging jobs will be done by women and will be part-time as well. This will lead not only to lower pay but to a situation in which companies will not have to pay benefits. Thus, the economic implications are found not only at the level of salary and working conditions, but at the level of support for health care, pensions, and so on. The ultimate public cost of this may be immense.

96. U.S. Department of Labor, *Outlook: 1990–2005*, p. 79.

97. Ibid., p. 80.

98. Russell Rumberger, "The Potential Impact of Technology on the Skill Requirements of Future Jobs," in Burke and Rumberger, eds., *The Future Impact of Technology on Work and Education*, p. 90.

99. See Apple, *Teachers and Texts*, and W. Norton Grubb, "Responding to the Constancy of Change: New Technologies and Future Demands on U.S. Education," in Burke and Rumberger, eds., *The Future Impact of Technology on Work and Education*, p. 122.

100. Apple, *Teachers and Texts*, especially Chapters 2 and 3.

101. Of course, women have organized to counter these threats and often will be successful in mediating and altering them. See Alice Kessler Harris, *Out to Work: A History of Wage-Earning Women in the United States* (New York: Oxford University Press, 1982). We should not assume that gender is a complete explanation here. This is also strongly related to the perceived economic imperatives for short-term profit and creating the "lean" corporation that is currently so popular. The fact that I.B.M., G.M., A.T.T., Sears Roebuck, and G.T.E. in the past 3 years announced layoffs of 325,000 employees in their aggressive pursuit of "down-sizing," documents this dynamic. See Richard J. Barnet, "Stateless Corporations," *The Nation* 259 (December 19, 1994), pp. 754–757.

102. See Michele Barrett, *Women's Oppression Today* (London: New Left Books, 1980). An excellent treatment of what young women experience in their paid and unpaid labor can be found in Christine Griffin, *Typical Girls* (London: Routledge, 1985). See also Heidi Safia Mirza, *Young, Female, and Black* (New York: Routledge, 1992). The issue of unpaid labor is linked to the wider question of identity. We may need a redefinition of work that is not totally tied into the capitalist economy, one in which the "labor of caring" that often is done by women is much more highly valued.

103. Chris Shilling, "Work Experience as a Contradictory Practice," *British Journal of Sociology of Education*, in press, p. 22.

104. Ibid., p. 9.

105. Ibid.

106. Ibid., p. 14.

107. Ibid.

108. Quoted in Lillian Rubin, *Worlds of Pain* (New York: Basic Books, 1976), p. 14.

109. Grubb, "Responding to the Constancy of Change," p. 130.

110. Ibid.

111. Gerald Burke, ''Reforming the Structure and Finance of Education in Australia,'' in Burke and Rumberger, eds., *The Future Impact of Technology on Work and Education*, p. 180. On the government's need to maintain legitimacy, especially in times of crisis, see Apple, *Education and Power*.

112. Ibid.

113. Christopher Jencks, ''Comment,'' in Danziger and Weinberg, eds., *Fighting Poverty*, pp. 176–177.

114. Nathan Glazer, ''Education and Training Programs and Poverty,'' in Danziger and Weinberg, eds., *Fighting Poverty*, p. 154.

115. Danziger, Haveman, and Plotnick, ''Antipoverty Policy,'' p. 75.

116. Useful here are Alec Nove, *The Economics of Feasible Socialism* (Boston: Allen & Unwin, 1983), Carnoy, Shearer, and Rumberger, *A New Social Contract*, Martin Carnoy and Derek Shearer, *Economic Democracy* (White Plains, NY: M.E. Sharpe, 1980), and Marcus Raskin, *The Common Good* (New York: Routledge, 1986). For interesting discussions of educational policies and practices, see Roger Simon, Don Dippo, and Arleen Schenke, *Learning Work: A Critical Pedagogy of Work Education* (New York: Bergin & Garvey, 1991), and Michael W. Apple and James A. Beane, eds., *Democratic Schools* (Washington, DC: Association for Supervision and Curriculum Development, 1995).

117. Hamilton and Hamilton, ''Social Policies, Civil Rights, and Poverty,'' p. 311. As we mentioned in note 102, however, this requires a serious questioning of what *counts* as a job. Most definitions privilege male definitions and give less attention to the work surrounding caring and connectedness that in many societies women usually do. Thus, we need to alter our very assumptions about labor and must support much greater diversity both ideologically and economically.

118. Raskin, *The Common Good*, p. 8.


CHAPTER 5

1. See Michael W. Apple, *Ideology and Curriculum*, 2nd edition (New York: Routledge, 1990), and Cameron McCarthy and Warren Crichlow, eds., *Race, Identity, and Representation in Education* (New York: Routledge, 1993).

2. Nancy Fraser and Linda Gordon, ''A Genealogy of Dependency,'' *Signs* 19 (Winter 1994), p. 311.

3. Geoff Whitty, ''Consumer Rights versus Citizen Rights in Contemporary Education Policy.'' Unpublished paper, University of London, Institute of Education, 1994, pp. 1–2.

4. Ibid., p. 13.

5. Ibid., p. 18.

6. Ibid., p. 21.

7. R. W. Connell, *Schools and Social Justice* (Philadelphia: Temple University Press, 1993), pp. 11–14.

8. Ibid., p. 14.

9. See, for example, Michael W. Apple, *Education and Power* (New York: Routledge, 1985). On the conversion strategies that are entailed in the social uses of such credentials, see Pierre Bourdieu, *Distinction* (Cambridge, MA: Harvard University Press, 1984).

10. Connell, *Schools and Social Justice*, p. 14.

11. Ibid., pp. 14–15. Italics in original.

12. Ibid., p. 15.

13. Quoted in James Donald, *Sentimental Education: Schooling, Popular Culture and the Regulation of Liberty* (New York: Verso, 1992), p. 17.

14. Ibid., pp. 55–57.

15. Jonathan Kozol, *Savage Inequalities* (New York: Crown, 1991).

16. See Apple, *Ideology and Curriculum*, and Michael W. Apple, *Official Knowledge: Democratic Education in a Conservative Age* (New York: Routledge, 1993).

17. Walter Secada, "Introduction," in Walter Secada, Elizabeth Fennema, and Lisa Byrd Adajian, eds., *New Directions in Equity for Mathematics Education* (New York: Cambridge University Press, 1995), pp. 4–5.

18. See Apple, *Education and Power*, and Jeannie Oakes, *Keeping Track* (New Haven: Yale University Press, 1985).

19. Donald, *Sentimental Education*, p. 122.

20. Apple, *Official Knowledge*.

21. See Michael W. Apple, *Teachers and Texts: A Political Economy of Class and Gender Relations in Education* (New York: Routledge, 1988).

22. John Dewey quoted in Ken Jones, *Right Turn: The Conservative Revolution in Education* (London: Hutchinson, 1989), p. 104.

23. Ontario Federation of Labour, "Education and Training," in Nancy Jackson, ed., *Training for What? Labour Perspectives on Skill Training* (Toronto: Our Schools/Our Selves Education Foundation, 1992), pp. 102–103.

24. Jim Turk, "If Training Is the Answer, What Is the Question?" in Nancy Jackson, ed., *Training for What?*, p. 5.

25. Ibid., p. 6.

26. Ibid.

27. Antonio Gramsci quoted in Jones, *Right Turn*, p. 104.

28. Jones, *Right Turn*, p. 104.

29. For a concrete example of how such connections can be made, see Roger Simon, Don Dippo, and Arleen Schenke, *Learning Work: A Critical Pedagogy of Work Education* (New York: Bergin & Garvey, 1991).

30. Judith Williamson quoted in Jones, *Right Turn*, p. 182.

31. Andy Hargreaves and David Reynolds, eds., *Educational Policies: Controversies and Critiques* (New York: Falmer Press, 1989), p. 22.

32. Linda McNeil, *Contradictions of Control* (New York: Routledge, 1986).

33. Gloria Ladson-Billings, *The Dreamkeepers* (San Francisco: Jossey-Bass, 1994).

34. Michelle Fine, "[Ap]parent Involvement: Reflections on Parents,

Power, and Urban Public Schools," *Teachers College Record* 94 (Summer 1993), p. 684.

35. Ibid., p. 69.

36. Ibid., pp. 691–692.

37. Ibid., p. 696.

38. See Apple, *Official Knowledge.*

39. Ibid., p. 692. Italics in original.

40. See, for example, Richard Herrnstein and Charles Murray, *The Bell Curve* (New York: Free Press, 1994).

41. See, for example, Michael W. Apple and James A. Beane, eds., *Democratic Schools* (Washington, DC: Association for Supervision and Curriculum Development, 1995), Gregory Smith, ed., *Public Schools That Work* (New York: Routledge, 1994), and Secada, Fennema, and Adajian, *New Directions in Equity for Mathematics Education.*

42. See Apple and Beane, *Democratic Schools*, and Apple, *Official Knowledge.*

43. Donald, *Sentimental Education*, p. 137.

44. Cornel West, *Race Matters* (New York: Vintage Books, 1993), p. 156.

45. See, for example, Michael Omi and Howard Winant, *Racial Formation in the United States*, 2nd edition (New York: Routledge, 1994).

46. Ibid., p. 150.

47. Ibid.

48. Fraser and Gordon, "A Genealogy of Dependency," p. 320.

49. Ibid.

50. Ibid., p. 324.

51. Ibid.

52. Ibid., pp. 324–325.

53. Ibid., p. 325.

54. Herrnstein and Murray, *The Bell Curve.*

55. Fraser and Gordon, "A Genealogy of Dependency," p. 331.

56. Michael B. Katz, *The Undeserving Poor* (New York: Pantheon, 1989), p. 239. I realize that democracy as a concept is a "sliding signifier" and in fact have argued such a case in *Official Knowledge*, where I show how it is constructed and used by different groups with very different agendas. However, theoretical elegance can sometimes get in the way of our ordinary insights about things that might bind us together to contest rightist reconstructions. That is my point here.

57. Ibid.

58. Ibid.

59. See Michael W. Apple and Lois Weis, eds., *Ideology and Practice in Schooling* (Philadelphia: Temple University Press, 1983), especially Chapter 1.

60. Apple and Beane, *Democratic Schools.* Also important here is Smith, *Public Schools That Work.*

61. Edward Said, *Culture and Imperialism* (New York: Vintage Books, 1993), p. 303.

# Bibliography

Apple, Michael W. *Education and Power*. New York: Routledge, 1985, 2nd edition, 1995.

Apple, Michael W. "Social Crisis and Curriculum Accords," *Educational Theory* 38 (Spring 1988), pp. 191–201.

Apple, Michael W. *Teachers and Texts: A Political Economy of Class and Gender Relations in Education*. New York: Routledge, 1988.

Apple, Michael W. *Ideology and Curriculum*, 2nd edition. New York: Routledge, 1990.

Apple, Michael W. *Official Knowledge: Democratic Education in a Conservative Age*. New York: Routledge, 1993.

Apple, Michael W. "Cultural Capital and Official Knowledge." In Michael Berube and Cary Nelson, eds., *Higher Education Under Fire*. New York: Routledge, 1994, pp. 91–107.

Apple, Michael W. "Texts and Contexts: The State and Gender in Educational Policy," *Curriculum Inquiry* 24 (Fall 1994), pp. 349–359.

Apple, Michael W. "Review of Ian Hunter, *Rethinking the School*," *Australian Journal of Education*, 39 (April 1995), pp. 95–96.

Apple, Michael W. and Beane, James A., eds. *Democratic Schools*. Washington, DC: Association for Supervision and Curriculum Development, 1995.

Apple, Michael W. and Christian-Smith, Linda, eds. *The Politics of the Textbook*. New York: Routledge, 1990.

Apple, Michael W. and Jungck, Susan. "You Don't Have to Be a Teacher to Teach This Unit," *American Educational Research Journal* 27 (Summer 1990), pp. 227–251.

Apple, Michael W. and Weis, Lois, eds. *Ideology and Practice in Schooling*. Philadelphia: Temple University Press, 1983.

Arnot, Madeleine. "Feminism, Education and the New Right." Unpublished paper presented at the American Educational Research Association, Chicago, 1991.

Barnet, Richard J. "Stateless Corporations," *The Nation* 259 (December 19, 1994), pp. 754–757.

Barrett, Michele. *Women's Oppression Today*. London: New Left Books, 1980.

Bastian, Ann, Fruchter, Norm, Gittell, Marilyn, Greer, Colin, and Haskins, Kenneth. *Choosing Equality*. Philadelphia: Temple University Press, 1986.

Bernstein, Basil. *Class, Codes and Control*, Volume 3. New York: Routledge, 1977.

Bernstein, Basil. *The Structuring of Pedagogic Discourse: Class, Codes and Control*, Volume 4. New York: Routledge, 1990.

Best, Steven and Kellner, Douglas. *Postmodern Theory: Critical Interrogations*. London: Macmillan, 1991.

Bhabha, Homi K. *The Location of Culture*. New York: Routledge, 1994.

Blank, Rebecca M. and Blinder, Alan, S. "Macroeconomics, Income Distribution, and Poverty." In Sheldon H. Danziger and Daniel Weinberg, eds., *Fighting Poverty: What Works and What Doesn't*. Cambridge, MA: Harvard University Press, 1986, pp. 180–208.

Bocock, Peter. *Hegemony*. New York: Tavistock, 1986.

Bourdieu, Pierre. *Distinction*. Cambridge, MA: Harvard University Press, 1984.

Burke, Gerald. "Reforming the Structure and Finance of Education in Australia." In Gerald Burke and Russell Rumberger, eds., *The Future Impact of Technology on Work and Education*. Philadelphia: Falmer Press, 1987, pp. 178–193.

Burtless, Gary. "Public Spending for the Poor: Trends, Prospects, and Economic Limits." In Sheldon H. Danziger and Daniel Weinberg, eds., *Fighting Poverty: What Works and What Doesn't*. Cambridge, MA: Harvard University Press, 1986, pp. 18–49.

Burtless, Gary, ed. *A Future of Lousy Jobs?* Washington: The Brookings Institution, 1990.

Carnoy, Martin and Levin, Henry. *Schooling and Work in the Democratic State*. Stanford: Stanford University Press, 1985.

Carnoy, Martin and Shearer, Derek. *Economic Democracy*. White Plains, NY: M. E. Sharpe, 1980.

Carnoy, Martin, Shearer, Derek, and Rumberger, Russell. *A New Social Contract*. New York: Harper & Row, 1983.

Cohen, Joshua and Rogers, Joel. *On Democracy: Toward a Transformation of American Society*. New York: Penguin Books, 1983.

Connell, R. W. *Schools and Social Justice*. Philadelphia: Temple University Press, 1993.

Coontz, Stephanie. *The Social Origins of Private Life*. New York: Verso, 1988.

Coontz, Stephanie. *The Way We Never Were*. New York: Basic Books, 1992.

Curtis, Bruce. *True Government by Choice Men?* Toronto: University of Toronto Press, 1992.

Dale, Roger. "The Thatcherite Project in Education," *Critical Social Policy* 9 (no. 3, 1989).

Danziger, Sheldon H., Haveman, Robert H., and Plotnick, Robert D. "Antipoverty Policy: Effects on the Poor and the Nonpoor." In Sheldon H. Danziger and Daniel Weinberg, eds., *Fighting Poverty: What Works and What Doesn't*. Cambridge, MA: Harvard University Press, 1986, pp. 50–77.

Danziger, Sheldon H. and Weinberg, Daniel, eds. *Fighting Poverty: What Works and What Doesn't*. Cambridge, MA: Harvard University Press, 1986.

Darling-Hammond, Linda. "Bush's Testing Plan Undercuts School Reforms," *Rethinking Schools* 6 (March/April, 1992), p. 18.

DeHart, Joan Sherron. "Gender on the Right: Behind the Existential Scream," *Gender and History* 3 (Winter 1991), pp. 246–267.

Delfattore, Joan. *What Johnny Shouldn't Read*. New Haven: Yale University Press, 1992.

Donald, James. *Sentimental Education: Schooling, Popular Culture and the Regulation of Liberty*. New York: Verso, 1992.

Droste, Kathleen, ed. *Gale Book of Averages*. Detroit: Gale Research Incorporated, 1994.

Eagleton, Terry. *Literary Theory*. Minneapolis: University of Minnesota Press, 1983.

*Economic Report of the President*. Washington, DC: U.S. Government Printing Office, 1994.

Education Group II, eds. *Education Limited*. London: Unwin Hyman, 1991.

Edwards, Tony, Gewirtz, Sharon, and Whitty, Geoff. "Whose Choice of Schools?" In Madeleine Arnot and Len Barton, eds., *Voicing Concerns: Sociological Perspectives on Contemporary Educational Reforms*. London: Triangle Books, 1992, pp. 143–162.

Ellsworth, Elizabeth. "Why Doesn't This Feel Empowering?" *Harvard Educational Review* 59 (August 1989), pp. 297–324.

Ellwood, David T. and Summers, Lawrence H. "Poverty in America." In Sheldon H. Danziger and Daniel Weinberg, eds., *Fighting Poverty: What Works and What Doesn't*. Cambridge, MA: Harvard University Press, 1986, pp. 78–105.

Feinberg, Walter. *Japan and the Pursuit of a New American Identity*. New York: Routledge, 1993.

Fine, Michelle. "[Ap]parent Involvement: Reflections on Parents, Power, and Urban Public Schools," *Teachers College Record* 94 (Summer 1993), pp. 682–710.

Fraser, Nancy. *Unruly Practices*. Minneapolis: University of Minnesota Press, 1989.

Fraser, Nancy and Gordon, Linda. "A Genealogy of Dependency," *Signs* 19 (Winter 1994), pp. 309–336.

Giroux, Henry. *Border Crossings*. New York: Routledge, 1992.

Giroux, Henry. "Doing Cultural Studies: Youth and the Challenge of Pedagogy," *Harvard Educational Review* 64 (Fall 1994), pp. 278–308.

Glazer, Nathan. "Education and Training Programs and Poverty." In Sheldon H. Danziger and Daniel Weinberg, eds., *Fighting Poverty: What Works and What Doesn't*. Cambridge, MA: Harvard University Press, 1986, pp. 152–172.

Gould, Stephen Jay. *The Mismeasure of Man*. New York: W. W. Norton, 1981.

Green, Andy. "The Peculiarities of English Education." In Education Group II, eds., *Education Limited*. London: Unwin Hyman, 1991, pp. 6–30.

Green, Francis and Sutcliffe, Bob. *The Profit System: The Economics of Capitalism*. New York: Penguin Books, 1987.

Griffin, Christine. *Typical Girls*. London: Routledge, 1985.

Grubb, Norton W. "Responding to the Constancy of Change: New Technologies and Future Demands on U.S. Education." In Gerald Burke and Russell Rumberger, eds., *The Future Impact of Technology on Work and Education*. Philadelphia: Falmer Press, 1987, pp. 118–140.

Hamilton, Charles V. and Hamilton, Dona C. "Social Policies, Civil Rights, and Poverty." In Sheldon H. Danziger and Daniel Weinberg, eds., *Fighting Poverty: What Works and What Doesn't*. Cambridge, MA: Harvard University Press, 1986, pp. 287–311.

Haraway, Donna. *Primate Visions*. New York: Routledge, 1989.

Harding, Sandra. *Whose Science, Whose Knowledge?* Ithaca, NY: Cornell University Press, 1991.

Harding, Sandra and Barr, Jean F., eds. *Sex and Scientific Inquiry*. Chicago: University of Chicago Press, 1987.

Hargreaves, Andy and Reynolds, David, eds. *Educational Policies: Controversies and Critiques*. New York: Falmer Press, 1989.

Harris, Alice Kessler. *Out to Work: A History of Wage-Earning Women in the United States*. New York: Oxford University Press, 1982.

Herrnstein, Richard and Murray, Charles. *The Bell Curve*. New York: Free Press, 1994.

Hirsch, E. D., Jr. *Cultural Literacy*. New York: Houghton Mifflin, 1986.

Honderich, Ted. *Conservatism*. Boulder: Westview Press, 1990.

Hunter, Allen. "The Politics of Resentment and the Construction of Middle America." Unpublished paper, Department of Sociology, University of Wisconsin, Madison, 1987.

Hunter, Allen. *Children in the Service of Conservatism*. Madison: University of Wisconsin, Madison Law School, Institute for Legal Studies, 1988.

Hunter, Ian. *Rethinking the School*. St. Leonards, Australia: Allen & Unwin, 1994.

International Bank for Reconstruction and Development/The World Bank. *Social Indicators of Development: 1994*. Baltimore, MD: Johns Hopkins University Press, 1994.

Jencks, Christopher. "Comment." In Sheldon H. Danziger and Daniel Weinberg, eds., *Fighting Poverty: What Works and What Doesn't*. Cambridge, MA: Harvard University Press, 1986, pp. 173–179.

Johnson, Richard. "A New Road to Serfdom." In Education Group II, eds., *Education Limited*. London: Unwin Hyman, 1991, pp. 31–86.

Johnson, Richard. "Ten Theses on a Monday Morning." In Education Group II, eds., *Education Limited*. London: Unwin Hyman, 1991, pp. 307–321.

Jones, Ken. *Right Turn: The Conservative Revolution in Education*. London: Hutchinson, 1989.

Jules, Didacus and Apple, Michael W. "The State and Educational Reform." In William Pink and George Noblit, eds., *The Futures of Sociology of Education*. Norwood, NJ: Ablex, 1995.

Karp, Stan. "Massachusetts 'Choice' Plan Undercuts Poor Districts," *Rethinking Schools* 6 (March/April 1992), p. 4.

Katz, Michael B. *The Undeserving Poor*. New York: Pantheon, 1989.

Klatch, Rebecca. *Women of the New Right*. Philadelphia: Temple University Press, 1987.

Koza, Julia. ''Rap Music,'' *The Review of Education/Pedagogy/Cultural Studies*, in press.

Kozol, Jonathan. *Savage Inequalities*. New York: Crown, 1991.

Kurian, George Thomas. *The New Book of World Rankings*. New York: Facts on File, 1991.

Kutscher, Ronald. ''The Impact of Technology on Employment in the United States.'' In Gerald Burke and Russell Rumberger, eds., *The Future Impact of Technology on Work and Education*. Philadelphia: Falmer Press, 1987, pp. 33–54.

Ladson-Billings, Gloria. *The Dreamkeepers*. San Francisco: Jossey-Bass, 1994.

Lewis, Jane. ''Back to the Future: A Comment on American New Right Ideas About Welfare and Citizenship in the 1980s,'' *Gender and History* 3 (Autumn 1991), pp. 326–336.

Liston, Daniel. *Capitalist Schools*. New York: Routledge, 1988.

Lowe, Robert. ''The Illusion of 'Choice,''' *Rethinking Schools* 6 (March/April 1992), pp. 1, 21–23.

Luke, Carmen and Gore, Jenny, eds. *Feminisms and Critical Pedagogy*. New York: Routledge, 1992.

Maguire, Kathleen, Pastore, Ann L., and Flanagan, Timothy J., eds. *Sourcebook of Criminal Justice Statistics: 1992*. Washington, DC: U.S. Government Printing Office, U.S. Department of Justice, Bureau of Justice Statistics, 1993.

McCarthy, Cameron and Crichlow, Warren, eds. *Race, Identity, and Representation in Education*. New York: Routledge, 1993.

McCloskey, Donald N. *The Rhetoric of Economics*. Madison: University of Wisconsin Press, 1985.

McGuigan, Jim. *Cultural Populism*. New York: Routledge, 1992.

McNeil, Linda. *Contradictions of Control*. New York: Routledge, 1986.

Mirza, Heidi Safia. *Young, Female, and Black*. New York: Routledge, 1992.

Nove, Alec. *The Economics of Feasible Socialism*. Boston: Allen & Unwin, 1983.

Oakes, Jeannie. *Keeping Track*. New Haven: Yale University Press, 1985.

Oliver, Anita. *The politics of textbook controversy: Parents challenge the implementation of a reading series*. Unpublished doctoral thesis, University of Wisconsin, Madison, 1993.

Omi, Michael and Winant, Howard. *Racial Formation in the United States*, 2nd edition. New York: Routledge, 1994.

Ontario Federation of Labour. ''Education and Training.'' In Nancy Jackson, ed., *Training for What? Labour Perspectives on Skill Training*. Toronto: Our Schools/Our Selves Education Foundation, 1992, pp. 102–103.

Raskin, Marcus. *The Common Good*. New York: Routledge, 1986.

Razack, Sherene. ''What Is to Be Gained by Looking White People in the Eye? Culture, Race, and Gender in Cases of Sexual Violence,'' *Signs* 19 (Summer 1994), pp. 894–923.

Reese, William. *Power and the Promise of School Reform*. New York: Routledge, 1986.

Robertson, David. "The Meaning of Multiskilling." In Nancy Jackson, ed., *Training for What? Labour Perspectives on Skill Training*. Toronto: Our Schools/Our Selves Education Foundation, 1992, pp. 29–42.

Roman, Leslie and Apple, Michael W. "Is Naturalism a Move Beyond Positivism?" In Elliot Eisner and Alan Peshkin, eds., *Qualitative Inquiry in Education*. New York: Teachers College Press, 1990, pp. 38–73.

Rose, Susan. *Keeping Them out of the Hands of Satan*. New York: Routledge, 1988.

Rubin, Lillian. *Worlds of Pain*. New York: Basic Books, 1976.

Rumberger, Russell. "The Potential Impact of Technology on the Skill Requirements of Future Jobs." In Gerald Burke and Russell Rumberger, eds., *The Future Impact of Technology on Work and Education*. Philadelphia: Falmer Press, 1987, pp. 74–95.

Said, Edward. *Culture and Imperialism*. New York: Vintage Books, 1993.

Schaeffer, Francis A. *The Francis A. Schaeffer Trilogy*. Westchester, IL: Crossway Books, 1990.

Schlesinger, Arthur M. *The Disuniting of America*. New York: Whittle Communications, 1991.

Schmittroth, Linda, ed. *Statistical Record of Women Worldwide*. Detroit: Gale Research Incorporated, 1994.

Secada, Walter. "Introduction." In Walter Secada, Elizabeth Fennema, and Lisa Byrd Adajian, eds., *New Directions in Equity for Mathematics Education*. New York: Cambridge University Press, 1995.

Secada, Walter, Fennema, Elizabeth, Adajian, Lisa Byrd, eds. *New Directions in Equity for Mathematics Education*. New York: Cambridge University Press, 1995.

Sherman, Arloc. *Wasting America's Future: The Children's Defense Fund Report on the Costs of Child Poverty*. Boston: Beacon Press, 1994.

Shilling, Chris. "Work Experience as a Contradictory Practice," *British Journal of Sociology of Education*, in press.

Simon, Roger, Dippo, Don, and Schenke, Arleen. *Learning Work: A Critical Pedagogy of Work Education*. New York: Bergin & Garvey, 1991.

Smith, Gregory, ed. *Public Schools That Work*. New York: Routledge, 1994.

Smith, Jessie Carnie and Johns, Robert L., eds. *Statistical Record of Black America*. Detroit: Gale Research Incorporated, 1995.

Smith, Marshall S., O'Day, Jennifer, and Cohen, David K. "National Curriculum, American Style: What Might It Look Like?" *American Educator* 14 (Winter 1990), pp. 10–17, 40–47.

Tuana, Nancy, ed. *Feminism and Science*. Bloomington: Indiana University Press, 1989.

Turk, Jim. "If Training Is the Answer, What Is the Question?" In Nancy Jackson, ed., *Training for What?* Toronto: Our Schools/Our Selves Education Foundation, 1992, pp. 1–7.

United Nations. *Statistical Yearbook.* New York: United Nations Department for Economic and Social Information and Policy Analysis, 1994.

U.S. Bureau of the Census. *Workers With Low Earnings: 1964–1990.* Washington, DC: U.S. Government Printing Office, Current Population Reports, Series P60–178, 1992.

U.S. Bureau of the Census. *Measuring the Effects of Benefits and Taxes on Income and Poverty: 1992.* Washington, DC: U.S. Government Printing Office, Current Population Reports, Series P60–186RD, 1993.

U.S. Bureau of the Census. *Money Income of Households, Families, and Persons in the United States: 1992.* Washington, DC: U.S. Government Printing Office, Current Population Reports, Series P60–184, 1993.

U.S. Bureau of the Census. *Poverty in the United States: 1992.* Washington, DC: U.S. Government Printing Office, Current Population Reports, Series P60–185, 1993.

U.S. Bureau of the Census. *Statistical Abstract of the United States: 1994.* Washington, DC: U.S. Government Printing Office, 1994.

U.S. Department of Labor, Bureau of Labor Statistics. *Outlook: 1990–2005.* Washington, DC: U.S. Government Printing Office, 1992.

Wacquant, Loic J. D. "Towards a Reflexive Sociology," *Sociological Theory* 7 (Spring 1989), p. 46.

Weinstein, Matthew. *Robot world: A study of science, reality, and the struggle for meaning.* Unpublished doctoral dissertation, University of Wisconsin, Madison, 1995.

West, Cornel. *Race Matters.* New York: Vintage, 1993.

Wexler, Philip. *Becoming Somebody.* New York: Falmer Press, 1992.

Whitty, Geoff. "Recent Education Reform: Is It a Post-Modern Phenomenon?" Unpublished paper presented at the Conference on Reproduction, Social Inequality, and Resistance, University of Bielefeld, Bielefeld, Germany, October 1–4, 1991.

Whitty, Geoff. "Education, Economy and National Culture." In Robert Bocock and Kenneth Thompson, eds., *Social and Cultural Forms of Modernity.* Cambridge: Polity Press, 1992.

Whitty, Geoff. "Consumer Rights versus Citizen Rights in Contemporary Education Policy." Unpublished paper, University of London, Institute of Education, 1994.

Whitty, Geoff, Edwards, Tony, and Gewirtz, Sharon. *Specialisation and Choice in Urban Education.* New York: Routledge, 1993.

Williams, Raymond. *Marxism and Literature.* New York: Oxford University Press, 1977.

Williams, Raymond. *The Year 2000.* New York: Pantheon, 1983.

Williams, Raymond. *Resources of Hope.* New York: Verso, 1989.

Willis, Paul. "Youth Unemployment: Thinking the Unthinkable." Unpublished paper, Wolverhampton Polytechnic, Wolverhampton, England, n.d.

Willis, Paul, with Jones, Simon, Canaan, Joyce, and Hurd, Geoff. *Common Culture.* Boulder: Westview Press, 1990.

Wilson, William Julius and Neckerman, Kathryn M. "Poverty and Family Structure." In Sheldon H. Danziger and Daniel Weinberg, eds., *Fighting Poverty: What Works and What Doesn't*. Cambridge, MA: Harvard University Press, 1986, pp. 232–259.

Wright Edelman, Marion. "Introduction." In Arloc Sherman, *Wasting America's Future: The Children's Defense Fund Report on the Costs of Child Poverty*. Boston: Beacon Press, 1994.

# Index

# About the Authors

**Michael W. Apple** is John Bascom Professor of Curriculum and Instruction and Educational Policy Studies at the University of Wisconsin, Madison. A former elementary and secondary school teacher and past president of a teachers union, he has worked with governments, educators, unions, and activist and dissident groups throughout the world to democratize educational research, policy, and practice. Among his many books are *Ideology and Curriculum, Education and Power, Teachers and Texts, Official Knowledge,* and *Democratic Schools.*

**Anita Oliver** teaches in the School of Education at La Sierra University.

**Christopher Zenk** is a doctoral student and educational activist at the University of Wisconsin, Madison.